# DRIVING ME CRAZY

## STORIES FROM THE ROAD

## BRUCE MOELLER

DriveCam Inc.
San Diego, California

Published by DriveCam Inc.
San Diego, California

Publisher's Cataloging-in-Publication Data
Moeller, Bruce.

Driving me crazy : stories from the road / Bruce Moeller. – San Diego, CA : DriveCam Inc., 2008.

p. ; cm.

ISBN: 978-0-9815568-0-2

1. Traffic accidents.  2. Traffic safety.  I. Title.

HE5614.M64 2008
363.125—dc22                                    2008922258

Project coordination by Jenkins Group, Inc
www.BookPublishing.com

Interior design by Diane Neumeister

Printed in the United States of America
12  11  10  09  08 • 5 4 3 2 1

# Contents

# Preface

I have six children. Five of them are still alive.

One, my 18-month-old daughter Katie, died needlessly and tragically in Seoul, South Korea, in 1985.

One day she was a healthy, happy, blonde-haired, blue-eyed little wonder—full of joy and life. The next day, and for every day thereafter, her crib was empty and I couldn't awaken from this nightmare that had become our family's new reality. The next day, I could still remember her smell and her touch. I ached for her smile and her hugs.

I couldn't stop worrying about whether she was scared or cold that night, or for most nights for years thereafter. I understood on a conceptual level that she had died, but on an emotional level, I just couldn't wrap my head around the concept that she didn't exist anymore—except in my memory. I had to give most of her things away, and I had to temporarily take down all of her pictures.

I had to move from the place where we had lived because the memories kept haunting me. On the long, blurry plane ride back from Seoul to the United States, I kept seeing her face outside the window of the plane. It was as clear as the clouds in the sky.

One year later, I returned to Seoul. I saw her playing outside in the snow. I saw her at the Walker Hill property, where we had lived, laughed and loved. I kept thinking of Katie and what had happened. Once the hospital in Seoul realized that they were responsible for my little girl's untimely death, they immediately cremated the body. I never did see her lifeless body. The only thing I received were her ashes.

For two years, I couldn't speak, think or talk to anyone about my loss, and the feelings surrounding it, because I would break down in tears. I was too embarrassed about that potential public display of emotion to want to experience it, even though everyone wanting to help me was genuinely considerate and concerned.

For three years, I kept trying to make a deal with the devil. I can't remember how many times I offered to trade my life for hers—if only hers could be returned. I still knew I was dreaming. If only I could find a way to roust myself from this awful, deep sleep, I would rush to her room to hold and kiss her just once more.

For four years, I couldn't laugh. I couldn't allow myself to see the interesting and wonderful parts of life. I couldn't allow them to impinge upon my senses because I wasn't allowed to enjoy those things when she could no longer do so herself.

I was wracked with guilt for having failed to protect her. I went through the "if only" logic chains innumerable times until those thought processes wore deep trenches in my brain.

> "What if I'd never taken that overseas assignment?"
> "What if we hadn't gone to Hong Kong where she caught the flu?"
> "What else could I have done to save her life?"
> "What if I were a better person?"

In the futile hope of finding something of value or some redemption in this whole mess that had become my reality, I questioned everything. For hours, weeks, months, even years, the inevitable conclusion kept creeping back into its unsettling ubiquity. The paths taken, the choices made and their inevitable consequences could never be replayed or relived. I slowly learned that in life there are no do-overs, no mulligans and no devils with whom to deal. The devil went down to Georgia, and he was willing to make a deal. But even he couldn't reset the history I had set for myself and my family.

They say, "Time heals what reason cannot." In time, I was finally able to be gracious about people celebrating my birthday. To my own surprise, I actually enjoyed it—twenty-one years later. Until then, no matter what the celebration, I was explicit and radical about not celebrating something that Katie never had the chance to do more than once.

Because of this loss, I came to realize that some of my other children had developed issues with attachment. I learned that the same thought that continually played in my mind also turned over and over in their young minds. Why let yourself love something when you're going to lose it anyway?

As the years slipped away, my family grew apart. My daughter's mother and I no longer knew one another and split many years ago. Each of us went our own particular ways in our own individual cities. The pain and the memories were too great. One of us wanted to replace the gaping hole in our hearts while the other wanted to never take that risk again. The same pain, the same refrain. Why let yourself love something when you're going to lose it anyway?

My life prior to our tragedy was an old, tired, shallow and unexamined life. It is one, however, that became miraculously reborn, rethought and retooled after her death. Prior to her death, I thought I was happy and fulfilled. I was unencumbered with that dose of reality that life eventually teaches you. And, as with any youthful inexperience, no one could ever have convinced me that my life was not just as it should be—filled with hopes and dreams of conquering all obstacles while achieving anything to which I set my uncluttered mind. Life was good, the sky was the limit. I had my health, my career, my beautiful young family and the American Dream. All to be pursued and enjoyed, albeit on another continent.

However, having survived this unfortunate and untimely death, I am here to tell you that Nietzsche was right when he said, "Whatever doesn't kill you might make you stronger."

I learned that life does go on. I learned that many good things can emerge from the gloomy depths of the sea of destruction and despair. I learned to love and trust. I learned to hope and believe in a better tomorrow. I became more insightful and more compassionate. I allowed myself to love and risk again through three tremendous new lives figuratively created from my little girl's ashes. My three youngest children, who were born long after Katie's death, created a new family for me. They became my new reality. They came into my life well after I thought I didn't, couldn't and shouldn't want to go on living. To my pleasure, they have become the light of my life and a main reason for my wanting to stay engaged in every facet of this game of life.

I have grown, learned and achieved things I would never have undertaken had my daughter's death not challenged me to learn, adapt and thrive in the face of adversity.

My life has continued. I have written books and articles. I have given speeches and appeared on television and radio. I have created and grown companies. And I've taught my little ones to read and play basketball and baseball. In fact, I've even created another die-hard Cubs fan who, hopefully, will learn his lessons of disappointment and heartbreak by virtue of living vicariously in the world of the Cubs' Friendly Confines, instead of the way I was forced to experience it.

My whole orientation to life—and my perspective of it—was forever and radically changed. There was no turning back.

I went from being a cocksure, self-reliant, winner-take-all conservative to a more cautious, skeptical, compassionate liberal. Position, power, money and status were replaced by reflection, introspection, environment and empathy. My world had changed and I had changed because of it.

I began to value life. I viewed it as a temporary status to be nurtured, extended and revered at all costs. Of course, everyone thinks they value life, but in reality, how many take it for granted? How many actually live for, and worry about, tomorrow as opposed to being in the moment today? This was now my new reality. This is why I had to write this book. And why I created DrivingMeCrazyStories.com. It is a place to share your stories, learn from others and help make our world a safer place.

# Acknowledgments

This book is dedicated to the memory of my sweet little Katie, who lost her young life in Seoul, South Korea in 1985. From the tragedy of a life never lived came lessons and wisdom harnessed on building and creating better and safer lives for all who remain.

I have the unique opportunity to be the head of a company called DriveCam. I have been lucky to have met many passionate and interesting people with a common dedication to preventing the death and destruction we have all too readily come to accept on our roads.

My own family has been supportive and tolerant of my moods and extreme personality. They've also allowed the demands on my time and energy as I embark upon this journey of creating a whole new industry dedicated to eliminating the behavior that causes risky driving.

The team at DriveCam has been *the* most professional, intelligent and selfless group I have ever encountered. They all share the common vision of saving lives while building an industry with zero tolerance for "accidents."

Special thanks go to Eric Cohen, who helped pull my manuscript and stories together into the collection you have in front of you. I appreciate his research, perseverance and editorial expertise.

The extent to which we can be successful is the extent to which we will have contributed in making the world a safer and better place—even if it means affecting only one life while averting one potential tragedy at a time.

~ Bruce Moeller

## Chapter 1

# Gone in an Instant—Casualties of the Road

Although I try to push my own personal memories to the background of my life, any one event, thought or comment can trigger them—at any moment, at any place, at any time. In one recent instance, many of the memories of losing my daughter came flooding back when a highly publicized automobile crash made the news. The case was dubbed the "Flower Girl Case." It was a tragically sad story involving a drunken driver who crossed the median and hit a limousine carrying a beautiful little girl returning home from a family wedding. The seven-year-old was killed instantly as she slept in the back seat. Her mother, frozen by that instant in time, could only sit and watch as the events slowly unfolded in front of her.

I am told the mother held her lifeless little girl for over an hour not wanting to let go or say goodbye. Having been in a similar situation, though many years ago, I couldn't stop the tears from flowing when I heard this story. In fact, every grown man and woman who knows this story cries just thinking about it.

As painful and as life-changing as my daughter's death was, I cannot even begin to imagine how devastating it must be to know you are the one responsible for a fatal collision. The young man who caused this senseless death was driving drunk. He was sentenced to twenty-five years in prison. But his sentence goes far beyond that. His never-ending nightmare is that he is forced to think about the lives he's changed each and every day, desperately wishing he had not caused that trauma.

And his was only one automobile crash in one city, in one state, on one day in the United States. Every year, there are almost 43,000 deaths on our roadways and 127,000 in the European Region[1]. That's 170,000 driving-related deaths each and every year, and that's not even counting Asia and other developing regions.

Another way to look at the impact of these incidents is the monetary loss. Nearly a half trillion dollars in property, casualty and workers' compensation loss occurs as a result of this worldwide devastation. That's $518 billion. Or expressed another way, that's $518,000,000,000. And that's only in the United States and the European Region. What about the rest of the world?

According to the World Health Organization (WHO), road traffic crashes kill 1.2 million people a year—or an average of 3,242 people each and every day. In addition, road traffic crashes injure or disable between 20 million and 50 million people a year. And, road traffic crashes rank as the eleventh leading cause of death and account for 2.1 percent of all deaths globally.[2]

## There Are No Accidents

But are these really accidents? I argue that they are not. These events do not just happen as an accident. They are predictable and they are preventable. These accidents do not need to occur.

Take two several-thousand-pound vehicles trying to occupy the same place at the same time. If the result is a tie, then certainly there will be physical damage to the vehicle, but there may also be human damage, and it might be fatal. If the incident is "lucky" enough not to be fatal, there is still damage to the humans, damage to the vehicles and damage to the psyche.

The word to keep in mind is "lucky." Blessed with good fortune. Occurring by chance. Keep these phrases in mind because the opposite phenomenon is also true. When we drive and take risks, whether we're cutting corners, rushing or multi-tasking without ever having received a ticket or bent a fender, we are subtly reinforcing the notion that we can behave in this irresponsible manner. Why? Because there are not now, never were before, and never will be (by extension) any bad things happening as a result of our risk-taking. The result is that this makes us supremely confident, bold and, yes, aggressive. This is all fine and well until our luck runs out. Or, our good fortune is gone.

And, as the statistics prove, our collective luck does run out. Eventually, the very sobering point is that, despite all of our collective best intentions by well-educated, responsible, licensed drivers with families and friends, houses and mortgages, hopes and dreams, the luck runs out for more than 465 of us in the U.S. and in the European Region each and every day. That's nineteen deaths an hour. That's one death every three minutes. And as I said before, that's only in the United States and the European Region.

## Immortality versus Risk

Everyone thinks they're immortal. There is a funny aspect to human nature that protects us against undue fear or hopelessness. We always assume that the terrible things we read and hear about are only for the other guy; they will not happen to us. What, me worry?

However, when Christopher Reeve got on his horse that fateful day, he was certainly not thinking that his life, and the lives of those around him would change forever. He never considered that his luck would run out. Riding horses was his passion, and a fear of riding them would have kept him from what he loved and did best.

Howard Hughes was a great aviator, yet crashing planes did not deter him from his passion. Nor did it slow down the millionaire aviator, Stephen Fossett, still lost in the southwest desert. Or the hundreds of people who attempt to scale Mount Everest or Mount McKinley each and every year.

This belief system, which acts as a defense mechanism to shield us from paralyzing fear, is also what allows us to move forward with a healthy positive attitude and engage in those things that make life interesting and worthwhile. These acts of courage and involvement become the fabric of life that weave a meaningful tapestry and provide context for the mundane and uneventful moments of our existence.

Paradoxically, this same positive mental attitude that provides protection from debilitating fear also introduces risk to our physical well-being. All under the mental fortress of "It will never happen to me."

But in my family's case, reality quickly hit when we discovered, through my daughter's death, that sometimes the unthinkable actually can happen, and not just to the other guy. Once we repatriated back to the United States, we needed to start constructing what would become of the rest of us. And what would become of the rest of our lives. After finding no devil with whom to make a deal for my daughter's safe return, and finally stabilizing my own life to a point of actually wanting to go on living, I progressed through the denial phase of the healing process. It is a phase that everyone must work through in their own individual way.

## The Phoenix Rising

Believe me, there are enough self-help books and seminars on the various stages of grief that my own personalized experiences cannot add to that body of knowledge. However, what I can tell you that is interesting and insightful—and impacts each and everyone of us—is that, like the phoenix rising out of the ashes, another life can emerge.

By overcoming fire, death and old age, the phoenix represents triumph over adversity and rebirth into glory, thereby providing hope and constancy. In my case, the story is one of triumph and hope. I survived and overcame fire and death (literally) and old age (metaphorically). I rose from the ashes and my new life emerged.

All in all, life is precious and worth living every moment to its fullest. After every dark cloud, there really is a clearing on the horizon. This was reinforced again when my family had to evacuate our home due to the San Diego wildfires. "What do we pack? What's important? What can we live without?"

The richness and fullness of every experience is priceless for what you can take out of it and carry with you. Internalize each and every moment as insight and armor against other experiences that will inevitably intersect with you as you go about the business of building your own version of a Norman Rockwell painting.

And, remember that the next time you are behind the wheel and you enter a construction zone or get cut off by that rude bastard in front of you, or you get that text message or hear that cell phone ring, try to discipline yourself that these hard life lessons will come soon enough. They'll arrive on their own without you opening the invitational door wider for them. Cars don't cause accidents. People do. Being on the receiving end of a fatal tragedy is hard enough; you don't want to be the responsible party inflicting such pain and trauma on others. I've lived through the loss of a life; I don't want you to have to go through that too.

---

[1] WHO European Region is defined as: Albania, Andorra, Armenia, Austria, Azerbaijan, Belarus, Belgium, Bosnia and Herzegovina, Bulgaria, Croatia, Cyprus, Czech Republic, Denmark, Estonia, Finland, France, Georgia, Germany, Greece, Hungary, Iceland, Ireland, Israel, Italy, Kazakhstan, Kyrgyzstan, Latvia, Lithuania, Luxembourg, Malta, Monaco, Montenegro, Netherlands, Norway, Poland, Portugal, Republic of Moldova, Romania, Russian Federation, San Marino, Serbia, Slovakia, Slovenia, Spain, Sweden, Switzerland, Tajikistan, The former Yugoslav Republic of Macedonia, Turkey, Turkmenistan, Ukraine, United Kingdom of Great Britain and Northern Ireland, Uzbekistan

[2] *World Report on Road Traffic Injury Prevention*, World Health Organization, 2004

## Chapter 2

# There Are No Accidents, Only Bad Choices

Dr. Margaret Chan, Director-General of the World Health Organization (WHO) recently remarked that "road traffic crashes are not 'accidents'" and urged society to challenge the notion that "they are unavoidable." Chan's comments coincided with the publication of a WHO report that revealed traffic injuries are the leading cause of death in people ages ten to twenty-four around the world—surpassing HIV/AIDS, respiratory infections, self-inflicted injuries, violence, tuberculosis, fires and war. As mentioned in the previous chapter, the annual cost of road injuries and fatalities is $518 billion. The numbers are staggering and the physical, financial and emotional toll on victims and their families are incalculable.

The numbers are only slightly better at the local level. United States Secretary of Transportation Mary E. Peters recently announced a nationwide drop in the number of road deaths. The two percent decline, the largest in fifteen years, has resulted in the lowest highway fatality rate on record of 1.42 deaths per 100 million vehicle miles traveled (42,642), compared to 1.45 deaths per 100 million vehicle miles traveled (43,510) the year before. During the same period, passenger car injuries dropped 6 percent from 2.7 million in 2005 to 2.54 million in 2006, and large truck injuries fell 15 percent.

Most significantly, fatalities of occupants of passenger vehicles— cars, SUVs, vans and pickups—continued a steady decline to 30,521, the lowest annual total since 1993. So we're getting better, right? Wrong.

As Secretary Peters said, "Even one death is too many."[1]

The statistics are encouraging, but the fact remains that 42,642 Americans died in traffic crashes in 2006 alone. Now consider that 58,148 troops were killed during the course of the entire Vietnam War. Realize further that nearly 120 human lives—mothers and fathers, brothers and sisters, sons and daughters—are cut short every single day as a result of traffic "accidents," and you quickly realize there is not yet reason to celebrate.

Despite Secretary Peters' announcement and the overall decline in highway fatalities, the U.S. is still behind other countries in road safety and remains one of the world's most dangerous places to drive. The Organization for Economic Cooperation and Development and the International Transport Forum have ranked the U.S. number forty-two— behind Australia, France, Germany, Japan and the United Kingdom—of the forty-eight countries it measured in terms of fatalities per capita.

## A False Sense of Security

WHO's report included a list of suggestions for developing countries to help them raise awareness of this epidemic, improve road conditions and make vehicles safer. In the U.S., Congress has proposed legislation—from graduated license laws and reduced speed limits to new vehicle safety sticker requirements and harsher penalties for drunken driving—to curb traffic fatalities. Manufacturers have also taken a lead in responding to this national catastrophe by introducing new safety technology and "smart" cars that warn drivers when a traffic signal is about to turn red, that protect operators from drifting into adjacent lanes and sound alarms when drivers appear to be falling asleep at the wheel. Older technologies, including antilock brakes, seat belts and air bags, also have increased the safety of vehicles. Yet, despite these efforts, collisions and fatalities still occur at alarming rates.

Why? Innovation does not take the place of solid judgment and skill behind the wheel. A research paper, titled "An Exploration of the Offset Hypothesis Using Disaggregate Data: The Case of Airbags and

Antilock Brakes," published in the *Journal of Risk and Uncertainty* (Volume 32, Issue 2) suggests drivers adapt to innovations that improve safety by becoming *less* vigilant about safety—not *more* vigilant—and confirms the role driver behavior plays in vehicle crashes. Although it may be hard to believe, safer cars support the behavioral concept of false positive reinforcement:

> *The idea is that an individual can drive recklessly, or even just a bit less responsibly, because the automobile is extra safe. Also because the driver has taken extra risks before and not endured the consequence of having had his or her luck run out resulting in a crash, he or she has a false sense of positive reinforcement.*

> *The feeling is, "I have followed closely many times before and it has never resulted in a crash; therefore, I obviously can do it safely where others of lesser skill or agility may need those extra two seconds of following distance."*

Now I'm not saying that safer cars cause people to take risks. Safer cars or not, the risks are there. I see them every day. In fact, more than 6 million audio and video recordings of actual risky driving behaviors across virtually every industry prove it. Every collision, or consequence, seen in these videos has been preceded by a risky driving behavior. These are not accidents. And we don't have to accept them. More importantly, we can change them.

A driver may have been following too closely, driving too fast for conditions, allowing herself to be distracted by passengers or zoning out when suddenly traffic slowed ahead of her. Suddenly, she comes upon a sharp curve or fails to see a passing motorist and collides. Feeling secure in her vehicle—and her skills as a driver—and with the reassurance of advanced safety technology on her side, she lets down her guard. An accident? No, a collision.

It's a known fact that a human being left to his or her own devices will push the limits until they break. He knows the rules of the road, but regularly dodges them when law enforcement is not present. As the old saying goes, you don't get what you expect; you get what you inspect.

## Trust and Verify

Understanding human nature is what propels my relentless passion to reduce risky driving behavior and improve the safety of fleets every day. Human nature can be changed. Crashes can be prevented.

But how do people change human nature? How do we get people to do what does not come naturally? One way is with coaches. Positive reinforcement. Carrots and sticks. It is common in today's world for people to have coaches or groups to hold them accountable for doing what they know is good for them and doing what they know they should do anyway.

For instance, at Jenny Craig's Weight Loss Centers, people have weigh-ins to positively reinforce the notion of seeing their progress in tangible numbers as they use discipline to change their eating behavior. The scrutiny of not achieving progress and the ensuing embarrassment is also a negative consequence to be avoided. As well, we all remember attending school where we regularly had pop quizzes and tests to verify we had read and absorbed the assigned material. In fact, before we even knew of grades, we would strive for that gold star on that task we had just accomplished. Yes, it all started a long, long time ago.

This same concept carries on throughout our daily lives. However, the whole notion of doing what is right and best for us, in the long term, flies in the face of basic human nature. Our brains and response systems are geared for positive, immediate and certain consequences. And they generally have to do with extension of the species. We tend to get the most pleasure from those things that have an immediate impact on keeping us alive and/or promoting reproduction. That is why that double cheeseburger with fries (of course) followed by a nice long nap to conserve and store energy is so appealing.

From a long-term perspective, however, that stuff will kill ya. The thought process here is that the potential heart attack is future and uncertain, and it never has happened to me before. Therefore, it's probably not going to happen to me and, if and when it does, I'll deal with it then. We rationalize the behavior we want to engage in now so that we don't have to delay that gratification. Why else would we want to super-size our fries with that order?

Now consider this human condition of immediate gratification in the application of several ton vehicles going 60, 80 or 100 miles per hour. Think of our cars as tools to fulfill our needs. We need to get to where we want to be as soon as possible. We need to get fed immediately. We need to get to work on time. Or we need to meet that special someone who might just become Mr. or Ms. Right.

## Trust Me

Except for the occasional police car we may happen to glimpse on our way to fulfill our needs, we put these potential lethal weapons in each of our hands based solely on the honor system. After all, we've all been trained, we all know what to do, we all (mostly) have driver's licenses, and we will behave in a responsible manner to the long-term benefit of ourselves and society. We will not take risks with our life or those of others.

So, if I'm like everyone else, you'll need to trust me. Trust me, even though it is against my human nature to drive my few thousand pound vehicle on the crowded highways and streets with my fellow human beings in the way I was trained and licensed without regard for my selfish personal whims and desires. Trust me to delay my own self-gratification for food, drink, companionship, money and ego while joining you on the highway. Trust me to block out my emotions, such as anger, aggressiveness and over-confidence, because I was taught and told and trusted to do so. Trust me.

There are few things I can think of that are more crazy and reckless than that and yet we all put on our "Trust Me" T-shirts each and every day as we buckle up and turn the ignition key. We wear those T-shirts proudly as we maneuver on and off the highway, around school buses and into intersections teeming with people and vehicles.

Oh yeah, and don't forget to trust me to buckle up, too, because it is in my own long-term best interest.

Can you think of any other thing we do in society that has more potential to create more death, destruction, misery and cost, and yet we simply trust one another to go against our own very natures to do the right thing?

Whether it be you and me driving to work, running errands or taking our children to school, we all trust one another. We also trust the men and women driving those school buses, delivery trucks and trash trucks with whom we share the roads. And the moving trucks, taxis, public buses, cement mixers, long-haul trucks and fleets of all shapes, sizes and weights.

Think about those fleet drivers. We want drivers to be safe on the roads and to feel secure when they are operating heavy equipment, transporting loads or hauling passengers. To this end, companies have invested in vehicles outfitted with advanced safety technology, they take the appropriate measures to maintain those vehicles and ensure drivers are properly trained to operate them safely. Still, vehicle damages, personal injury, workers' compensation and claims costs continue to rise each year. Why? Because professional drivers have a false sense of security, they're human, and this is leading them to take greater risks behind the wheel.

## Root Causes

Do you actually see how your fleet drivers drive? Do you see the risks they take? Or, are they professional only during a ride-along situation? How sure are you that they follow the rules of your organization, not to mention the rules of the road?

Consider these root causes when considering how professional your drivers really are. And, learn how you can know who is a risky driver and how you can prevent him or her from causing a potential incident.

## Distractions

Distractions are common while driving. A driver's attention may be divided between driving, navigating, talking to passengers and other activities. Distractions can cause crashes. Some common distractions include:

- Cell phones
- Mapping/navigation
- Food or drink
- Passengers
- Other work tasks

## Poor Awareness

Safe driving requires active, effective information gathering. Potential threats must be identified early to avoid the abrupt, late decisions that so often create problems in traffic. Poor awareness is often at the root of risky driving situations. Some of these include:

- Not looking far enough ahead
- Blank stare
- Not scanning roadway

- Intersection not scanned
- Mirrors not checked
- Blind area not checked

## Demeanor

Demeanor means "behavior toward others." This is a subjective category, but consider it when considering your drivers. Examples include:

- Judgment error
- Blind area not checked
- Somewhat aggressive
- Aggressive
- Willful misconduct
- Drowsy/falling asleep

## Risky Actions

Although these actions may not influence the way someone drives, they are paramount to driver safety, particularly if a crash does occur. Examples include:

- Driver unbelted
- Passenger unbelted

## Fundamentals

These categories involve the fundamentals of safe driving and go to the very root of most collisions. Drivers who continually exhibit poor fundamentals are "a crash waiting to happen," and are a liability to your organization, as well as a hazard to others on the road. Some of these include:

- Following too closely
- Unsafe speed
- Traffic violation
- Failure to keep an out
- Poor lane selection
- In other's blind area

Yes, trust is a very good thing and it is essential in forming good solid relationships, but when it comes to driving, there really is an evil empire out there. Verification can defeat the Mr. Hyde in each and every one of us.

## CHEW ON THIS

**The following information is taken from the *World Report on Road Traffic Injury Prevention*, the first report on the subject developed jointly by WHO and the World Bank.**

- Road traffic crashes kill 1.2 million people a year or an average of 3242 people every day.
- Road traffic crashes injure or disable between 20 million and 50 million people a year.
- Road traffic crashes rank as the 11th leading cause of death and account for 2.1% of all deaths globally.
- 90% of road traffic deaths occur in low-income and middle-income countries.
- Countries in the WHO Western Pacific Region and the WHO South-East Asia Region account for more than half of all road traffic deaths in the world.
- More than half of all road traffic deaths occur among young adults between 15 and 44 years of age.
- 73% of all road traffic fatalities are male.
- Road traffic injuries are predicted to become the third largest contributor to the global burden of disease by 2020.
- Road traffic deaths are predicted to increase by 83% in low-income and middle-income countries, and to decrease by 27% in high-income countries. These figures amount to a predicted global increase of 67% by 2020.
- It is estimated that every year, road traffic crashes cost:
  - US $518 billion globally
  - US $65 billion in low-income and middle-income countries, exceeding the total amount received in development assistance
  - Between 1% and 1.5% of gross national product in low-income and middle-income countries
  - 2% of gross national product in high-income countries
  - Road traffic injuries put significant strain on health care budgets

---

[1] DOT 72-07, issued July 23, 2007, "Declining Traffic Deaths Lead to Lowest Highway Fatality Rate Ever Recorded, U.S. Transportation Secretary Mary E. Peters Announces."

## Chapter 3

# Who'd a Thunk It? Henry Ford's Real Legacy

Cue the dream music and rev up the time machine.

We're going to go back in our imaginations to the time of Henry Ford and his contemporaries trying to develop their "Iron Horses," which would replace real horses for the privileged and the wealthy.

Imagine what it must have been like to live in a world that revolved around small rural towns, their surrounding farms and the local church. We're talking early 1900s. Very early. During this time, traveling was a genuine ordeal involving a real live horse and carriage. If you really wanted to go somewhere, you had to pack a lunch, water for the horse, tools to repair the carriage tires and liniment to rub on those sore muscles at the end of the day. For you and for the horse.

There were no real roads, no pavement, no gas stations, no mini marts and no cell phones—not even a McDonald's. The children didn't have DVD entertainment systems to occupy them, the parents had no radios or BlackBerry's® to divert their attention. Microwave ovens, satellite dishes and iPods® were all visions of some man-made future society that no one could even begin to fathom.

It's an ugly thought!

But it was enough to get early entrepreneurs, like Henry Ford, to decide that there had to be a better way to move people from one place to another—quickly and cleanly. A way to travel where someone's life would not be in danger each time he or she took to the road. And an opportunity for anyone, of any means, to own a vehicle of his own.

In those days, you couldn't just pop out a business plan from your personal computer, and e-mail it to 200 venture capitalists to see who would invest in your vision. Things moved at a much slower pace back then. It took passion and vision, along with faith and commitment. As Henry famously said, "If I had listened to what people said they wanted, I would have designed a faster horse." I wasn't there, of course, but in my imagination, the earliest conversations with the future motor industry moguls and their prospective investors might have gone something like this:

> "Thanks for seeing me and looking at my machine that will revolutionize travel and actually replace horses someday," opens Henry.

> "How long have you hated animals, son?"

> "I don't hate animals at all. I just see a better, faster, cheaper way to get from here to there."

> "But there are no roads, and what do you feed 'em?"

> "They can travel on the ruts worn into the ground by the carriages and they run on oil! That's part of the beauty of this. You can get a gallon of that stuff for a penny or two and it'll run for miles on that gallon. It's cheap and it's plentiful. It's just lying in the ground and it'll never cost more than a nickel a gallon."

> "OK, I buy that part. But that machine will be expensive to make and only a few of the wealthiest people will ever be able to buy one. Son, you've got to think about markets that can reach thousands of people, not just dozens."

"This part is even better than the oil part. I'm going to pay my workers enough money so that they can buy them too. This will help create demand and effectively create a middle class!"

"Son, how long have you been a communist?"

Stop the music and fast forward back to the present.

How could Henry Ford have possibly envisioned that his Iron Horse would someday create millions of miles of paved roads, hundreds of thousands of gas stations and roadside motels, along with restaurants and all of the commerce and growth that went with it? And what would old Henry think about each family owning two or three cars (on average)?

With all of the economic growth, benefit and infrastructure creating hundreds of new industries and thousands of new businesses, also came the part that nobody could have, or would have, envisioned. The downside.

In 2004, there were approximately 835 million vehicles in the world clogging nearly every major artery leading to our huge and crowded cities. That's 835 million vehicles creating miserable traffic jams, short tempers, and ever-increasing diversions built into the equation. And this number is expected to grow to 1.1 billion by 2019. That would be an increase of 265 million vehicles—nearly the total number of vehicles on U.S. roads today—in only fifteen years. In fact, it's predicted that the industry will crank out more vehicles in the next twenty years than the 1.8 billion it built in its first 110 years.[1]

Now that we are ironically getting from here to there faster and better than we used to by horse and carriage, we have to wait in long lines of traffic for hours to complete our journey. What do we do to pass the time? We create diversions, such as eating and drinking, along with entertainment and efficiency devices.

Enter major new industries to accommodate this new need. We have fast food and drive-through coffee. We play with Nintendo and watch DVD movies. We listen to satellite radio, smoke cigarettes, shave and talk and text on cell phones. All while driving.

An unintended consequence of 835 million vehicles jamming up the world's roads with wonderful diversions making all this travel more enjoyable (or at least tolerable) is:

- 1.2 million annual fatalities
- 50 million injuries (that's 50,000,000)
- 500 million unsafe acts or near misses (that's 500,000,000)
- costing $518 billion in property and casualty loss (that's $518,000,000,000)

I included the actual numbers so you can see the magnitude of what this vision hath wrought. The statistics are bad enough. The raw numbers are staggering.

## A Glimpse at the Bottom of the Pyramid

These figures are not surprising. In fact, they're exactly in line with the findings of H.W. Heinrich, an executive with Travelers Insurance Company. In the 1930s, Heinrich studied over 75,000 injuries in the workplace in an effort to better understand cause. His conclusion was that most accidents would be preventable if only the acquired behavior of individuals could be changed. His Domino Theory of Accident Causation states that an accident is only one of a series of factors, each of which depends on a previous factor in the following manner:

1. Accident causes an injury.
2. Individual's negligent act or omission, or a faulty machine, causes an accident.
3. Personal shortcomings cause negligent acts or omissions.
4. Heredity and environment cause personal shortcomings.

Through his research, Heinrich determined that for every 300 unsafe acts, there are twenty-nine minor injuries and one serious injury. As it relates to driving, this means that most collisions are not the result of a one-time mistake, but rather, they are the ultimate consequence of repeating risky driving behaviors.

For instance, a friend of mine was recently involved in a rear-end collision. She was in fairly heavy freeway traffic and failed to stop in time when traffic ahead came to a standstill. Fortunately, no one was seriously injured, but the incident did result in front-end damage to my friend's car and minor damage to the back of the other vehicle. At least one occupant from the other vehicle submitted medical bills. And several thousands of dollars will change hands before all of the dust settles from this minor incident.

What was the cause? We'll never know for sure, but my friend told me that she had a misbehaving child in the back seat. The moment she turned around to look back and deal with the child was exactly the moment the car ahead jammed on its brakes. By the time she looked forward again, there was not enough time or space to stop. Was it bad luck? Or was it predictable and even preventable?

The fact is that my friend is always following too closely and reacting late. While riding with her, I find myself constantly pressing my foot against an imaginary brake pedal on the floorboard in an unconscious effort to get her to brake sooner. To make matters worse, she is usually doing something else while driving. Cell phone. Makeup. Lunch. No wonder a quick glance to her child had such a high cost. The frequent mixture of limited space and distracted driving made this incident inevitable.

Which brings us back to H.W. Heinrich. My friend's risky behaviors perfectly demonstrate the unsafe acts found at the bottom of "Heinrich's Pyramid."

Most people don't realize that, for many of us, the most dangerous part of the workday may be the commute. For others, their job may rank as one of the deadliest—particularly those where driving is a major part of their day. In fact, drivers (truckers and salespeople) rank as the ninth deadliest job in America with twenty-seven deaths per 100,000 workers. "On an absolute basis (as opposed to a per capita basis), highway fatalities are the number one killer on the job; most accidents stem from tired drivers veering off the road, rather than from multi-car accidents," stated the Bureau of Labor Statistics in their September 18, 2007 report.

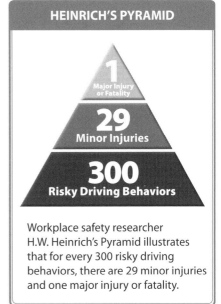

**HEINRICH'S PYRAMID**

**1** Major Injury or Fatality

**29** Minor Injuries

**300** Risky Driving Behaviors

Workplace safety researcher H.W. Heinrich's Pyramid illustrates that for every 300 risky driving behaviors, there are 29 minor injuries and one major injury or fatality.

Most fleet operators have little ability to dramatically reduce their crash frequency or claims costs because they only have knowledge of the top of the pyramid. Only when the accident report hits their desk do they have the means to identify problem drivers and launch into a driver improvement program.

The key to reducing the incidents at the top of the pyramid is to reduce the number of unsafe acts at the bottom of the pyramid. By identifying unsafe acts, you can address and correct them before they lead to traffic collisions. Those safety results not only save lives, but improve the bottom line, too.

Yet, no matter how much we focus on the bottom of the pyramid, incidents continue at the top of the pyramid. Over 1.2 million times, as stated previously. I'm sure Henry Ford would never have imagined this type of carnage. Nor, would he have believed H.W. Heinrich. But, the facts are the facts. From year to year. Country to country.

But, not to worry. This toll on human life has spawned new industries to repair the cars and the people. For instance, new industries have emerged to insure them against future loss. Now we can reconstruct what actually happened and determine who was at fault when those 835 million cars and trucks run into one another 50 million times. And new industries have been created to litigate against whoever was paying the least attention while driving and assign responsibility for the mess they created.

Oh, and at least one more industry has come on board ... driver risk management. Driver risk management programs exist to:

- Take risk out of driving.
- Reduce the frequency and also the severity of all those unsafe driving behaviors.
- Objectively report the truth as to what actually happened when an accident or fatality unfortunately occurred.

I'm sure Henry Ford could never have imagined the day when his invention could result in so much chaos and confusion, along with so much benefit to society. Nor could he have imagined the day when video event recorders could see inside and outside vehicles so we would know exactly what occurred in those few critical seconds immediately before and after an incident.

So there is both a cost and an opportunity that arises with innovation. Who'd a thunk it?

---

### HENRY FORD QUICK FACTS

**Henry Ford was a complex and, at times, contradictory personality with a wide range of interests and strongly held opinions. You probably know about Ford's achievements in automobile production, but did you know he also…**

- Built and drove race cars early in his career to demonstrate that his engineering designs produced reliable vehicles?

- Financed a pacifist expedition to Europe during WWI?

- Adopted a paternalistic policy to reform his workers' lives both at home and at work?

- Was an unsuccessful candidate for the United States Senate in 1918?

- Owned a controversial newspaper, *The Dearborn Independent*, which published anti-Jewish articles that offended many and tarnished his image?

- Promoted the early use of aviation technology?

- Built Village Industries, small factories in rural Michigan , where people could work and farm during different seasons, thereby bridging the urban and rural experience?

- Sought ways to use agricultural products in industrial production, including soybean-based plastic automobile components such as his experimental automobile trunk?

- Was one of the nation's foremost opponents of labor unions in the 1930s and was the last automobile manufacturer to unionize his work force?

- Mobilized his factories for the war effort and produced bombers, Jeeps and tanks for World War II?

- Established schools in several areas of the country that provided educational experiences based on traditional one room school techniques, modern teaching methods, and "learning through doing"?

- Established an indoor/outdoor museum — The Henry Ford — to preserve historical items that illustrated the American experience and American ingenuity?

## Which Came First? Roads or the Automobile?

Just over a century ago, steamships, canals, railroads and the telegraph were up and running. They were the technological marvels of the nineteenth century—setting the stage for the twentieth century. Yet the invention that would spark a revolution in transportation was a simple two-wheeler—the bicycle. Its popularity in the 1880s and 1890s spurred interest in the nation's roads.

On October 3, 1893, General Roy Stone, a Civil War hero and good roads advocate, was appointed special agent in charge of the new Office of Road Inquiry (ORI) within the Department of Agriculture. With a budget of $10,000, ORI promoted new rural road development to serve the wagons, coaches and bicycles on America's dirt roads.

At this same time, two bicycle mechanics in Springfield, Massachusetts, the Duryea brothers, built the first gasoline-powered "motor wagon" to be operated in the United States. Lacking any brakes on its historic first run in September 1893, the vehicle was brought to a stop by simply driving it into a curb. The Duryea brothers' success was little noted at the time, but it got the wheels turning for the introduction of the automobile, which would literally change the landscape of America.

In 1908, Henry Ford introduced his low-priced, highly efficient Model T. Its widespread popularity created pressure for the federal government to become more directly involved in road development. With rural interests adding to the battle cry of "Get the farmers out of the mud!" Congress passed the Federal-Aid Road Act of 1916. The act created the Federal-Aid Highway Program under which funds were made available on a continuous basis to state highway agencies to assist in road improvements. But before the program could get off the ground, the United States entered World War I.

Things took off again in the roaring '20s when the Bureau of Public Roads (BPR), as ORI was then called, was authorized by the Federal Highway Act of 1921 to provide funding to help state highway agencies construct a paved system of two-lane interstate highways. During the 1930s, BPR helped state and local governments create Depression-era road projects that would employ as many workers as possible. When America entered World War II in 1941, the focus turned toward providing roads that the military needed. After the war, the nation's roads were in disrepair, and congestion had become a problem in major cities. In 1944, President Franklin D. Roosevelt signed legislation authorizing a network of rural and urban express highways called the "National System of Interstate Highways." Unfortunately, the legislation lacked funding. It was only after President Dwight D. Eisenhower signed the Federal-Aid Highway Act of 1956 that the interstate program got under way.

From the start, the interstate system was hailed as the "Greatest Public Works Project in History"—a challenge embraced by several generations of highway engineers. But even more challenges were forthcoming. In the 1960s, BPR began to focus increasingly on environmental concerns and on creating urban road networks that tied into other land-use plans and transportation options, including mass transit. By 1966, the changing times prompted legislation to establish the U.S. Department of Transportation (DOT). When the new department opened in April 1967, BPR, renamed the Federal Highway Administration (FHWA), was one of the original components.

Throughout the 1970s and 1980s, FHWA worked with the states to open 99 percent of the designated 42,800-mile interstate system—now officially called the Dwight D. Eisenhower National System of Interstate and Defense Highways.

---

[1] Green Car Congress, July 2004

## Chapter 4

# Cars Don't Kill, Drivers Do

So we've established that there are nearly 43,000 fatalities annually on the highways and byways of the United States due to vehicular collisions. And, another 127,000 fatalities annually on the highways and byways of the European Region.

That's 465 human lives lost every single day of the year with no time off for holidays, vacations or interludes of any kind.

As they say, death takes no holiday.

Death is inevitable, but it can be temporarily cheated or delayed, postponed or put off, stalled or suspended. But can it be prevented?

Sometimes when someone "cheats" death, they do it by the pure luck of the trajectory of the carnage. A major organ or artery is spared by virtue of a few centimeters to the right or to the left of where the projectile entered the body.

We've also established that this "good luck" in cheating death and not becoming one of the 43,000 unfortunates in this year's U.S. graduating class, happens about twenty-nine times to every one fatality. That means luck played a factor in our avoiding death on the roads in 1,247,000 incidents.

But then, of course, there is the damage to one or both vehicles involved in each of those 1,247,000 mishaps. Add in the lost time for the human and the vehicle to remain on the sidelines, along with the workers' compensation costs, and you have an annual expense in the United States, alone, totaling a staggering $245 billion. Yes, that's billion with a "B."

To put it in a homeland security perspective, if all of those tragic deaths occurred in one place and at one time, it would be fourteen times the magnitude of what transpired on that infamous fall day in New York City, Washington, D.C., and Shanksville, Pennsylvania, in 2001.

Unlike natural death, however, when the Grim Reaper pays his inevitable visit at the end of a life cycle, these traffic fatalities are swift and cruel. Car crashes are the leading cause of death in teenagers, and this is especially brutal to their surviving friends and family because of the unfulfilled promise of the bright future they never had.

## They Die Too Young

Although traffic fatalities don't discriminate, they take a much harder toll on young drivers than the public at-large. For instance, teen drivers (sixteen to nineteen years old) have crash rates per mile driven that exceed those of drivers of any other age group, with sixteen-year-olds having the highest crash rates of all[1]. As many as 3,490 teen drivers (aged fifteen to twenty years old) were killed, and 272,000 reportedly injured in motor vehicle crashes in 2006[2]. This amounts to approximately one third of deaths from all causes for teenagers. Here is more grist for the mill:

- Motor vehicle crashes are the leading cause of death for teens in the United States, accounting for 41 percent of teen fatalities.
- More teens die in car crashes than the next four causes *combined*.[3]

It's easy to focus only on the teen driving problem because it's so large and so preventable. However, it's only one portion of the overall incident rate. All of this destruction is un-reconcilable, irreverent, unnecessary and costly in monetary terms, as well as in stress and emotion.

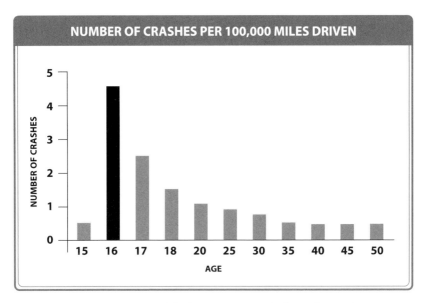

- In 2003, 5,240 teens were killed in passenger-vehicle crashes, and 458,000 teens were injured.[1]
- Driver fatalities for 15–20 year olds increased by 5 percent between 1994 and 2004.[1]
- During 2003, a teen died in a traffic crash an average of once every hour on weekends.[1]
- Sixty-three percent of the fatally injured 16–20-year-old passenger vehicle occupants were not wearing seatbelts, compared to 55 percent for adults 21 or older.[2]
- Crashes involving young drivers typically are single-vehicle crashes, primarily run-off-the-road crashes that involve driver error and /or speeding.[3]
- The presence of passengers strongly increases crash risk for teenage drivers; the more passengers the greater the risk.
- The crashes of youthful drivers are more likely to involve a single vehicle, driver error, and speeding.
- In 2000, 63 percent of the deaths of 13–19 year-old passengers occurred when other teenagers were driving.[4]

[1] *National Highway Transportation Safety Administration (NHTSA) Report —* **Teens at Risk.pdf**
[2] *NHTSA Report — Teenagers and Seatbelt Use*
[3] *Insurance Institute for Highway Safety (IIHS) —* **Crash Statistics**
[4] *IIH — "Teenage Passengers in Motor Vehicle Crashes; A Survey of Current Research," December 2001*

| CAUSES OF DEATH (15–19 YEARS OLD) | | |
|---|---|---|
| **RANK** | **CAUSE OF DEATH** | **% OF DEATHS** |
| **1** | **Motor Vehicles** | **41.4%** |
| 2 | Homicide | 13.7% |
| 3 | Suicide | 11.0% |
| 4 | Other Accidents | 10.3% |
| 5 | Cancer | 5.2% |
| 6 | Heart Disease | 2.9% |
| 7 | Genetic Diseases | 1.8% |
| 8 | Lung Disease | 0.7% |
| 9 | Flu/Pneumonia | 0.5% |
| 10 | Other | 11.8% |

- Teens are nine times more likely to be in a car crash than their parents
- The crash rate increases 700% when teens are not driving with their parents

*Teenage Drivers: Patterns of Risk*, Journal of Safety Research, 2003 (15 year old rate estimated by comparing crash rates of 15 year olds with a learner's permit with those of 16 and 17 year olds with full licenses)

Although we do not generally think in terms of 289 million vehicles in the U.S. (9 million fleet and 280 million personal vehicles) running around smashing into one another, and the unintended consequences of that chaos, we recognize that crashes do happen. That is why we require insurance. It is a way to force society to anticipate financial consequences for the inevitable death and destruction that will occur as we go about our daily lives commuting to and fro.

## Preventing the Inevitable

Here is where I want to challenge conventional thinking. Are these incidents really inevitable? If we can anticipate financial consequences based upon empirical data and project these onto an expected simulation of the future, why can't we do the same thing with the behaviors that cause the crashes in the first place? Why can't we anticipate them and then either reduce or eliminate them?

First, recall that for every one fatality there are twenty-nine incidents. Therefore we have thirty data points where we know factually that something happened, resulting in injury or death and certainly causing damage or destruction of property. How do we know this?

We have the actual physical damage to both person and property to prove that at least two physical entities attempted to occupy the exact same space at the exact same time, but the contest resulted in a tie. In traffic, when ties happen, everybody loses.

Just as the National Rifle Association contends that "Guns don't kill, people do," I contend that, with the rarest exception of a malfunction of the vehicle, "Cars don't kill, drivers do."

We see risky driving behaviors all the time. Every time we enter or exit the highway. Each time we change lanes. And every time we park our cars. In tens of thousands of instances every day, every week and every month of the year, we see them all around us.

Maybe it's a driver distracted by eating or drinking. Or, maybe he or she is speaking on a cell phone. Or maybe, he or she is eating, drinking *and* speaking on a cell phone.

Others are far more subtle, but nonetheless real.

We see the blank stare, which is basically a loss of concentration or failure to remain "in the moment."

Another frequent risky behavior is the failure to anticipate or look ahead to see what might happen to cause you to have to react quickly. How many times has a car started to turn in front of the car in front of you, but the driveway was blocked by a pedestrian, causing the car in front of you to have to stop to wait for the car in front of him to complete his turn and get out of the way? You know what I mean. If you don't anticipate this chain of events, you will have to course correct abruptly at the last moment. If you have time.

This leads to another high-risk behavior, which is not leaving an out. If, in the above scenario, you simply didn't have enough time to brake, and if you also had nowhere to go to swerve out of the path of the car in front of you, the result of that chain of unfortunate events is a collision.

Or how many times have you found other drivers (or even your-self) driving in the "No-Zone"? The Federal Motor Carrier Safety Administration (FMCSA) describes the "No-Zone" as the danger areas around trucks and buses where crashes are more likely to occur. According to the FMCSA, "some No-Zones are actual blind spots or areas around trucks and buses where your car 'disappears' from the view of the drivers. These blind spots are the Side No-Zone, Rear No-Zone and Front No-Zone areas," as depicted in the following illustration. Each time you drive in these areas, you are putting yourself at risk for a vehicle collision.

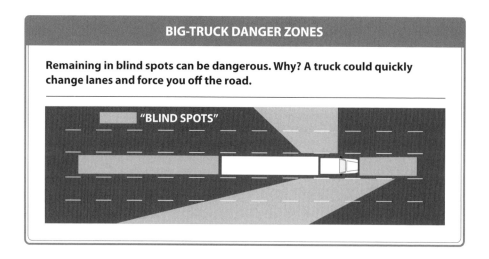

**BIG-TRUCK DANGER ZONES**

Remaining in blind spots can be dangerous. Why? A truck could quickly change lanes and force you off the road.

"BLIND SPOTS"

## Luck Be a Lady Tonight ... and Every Night

Would it surprise you to learn that for every one death and twenty-nine incidents, there are at least ten to fifteen risky behaviors that could have, or would have, resulted in a tie with another vehicle or person except for one small factor, *pure luck!*

By pure, unadulterated luck, in those ten to fifteen instances of risky driving behavior, that motorist won or lost the race for the same space at the same time. More importantly, or *luckily*, those same risky behaviors did not result in death and destruction.

Does this sound strange to you? Does it intrude on your existing beliefs that collisions are by definition accidents because they were unavoidable? In point of fact, all but the most extremely rare occurrences of mechanical failure are predictable and preventable.

Let me approach my argument from another perspective. When you see a collision, do you think that the root cause of the crash—the risky driving behavior itself—was exhibited just this one and only time?

I suppose in the world of theoretical possibilities, it is a mathematical possibility that the one and only time a driver exhibited a particular risky behavior, it resulted in a crash the very first and only time it ever happened. That possibility exists, however, only in theory. Why? Because in practice, all behaviors are learned, and they are learned as a result of no negative consequences following the risky behavior.

If every single time I was speeding in my car, I crashed, I would quickly learn cause and effect. And, as a consequence of the negative and certain crashes, I would condition myself not to speed in the future. Alternatively, if I never crash when I speed, I may falsely conclude that speeding does not cause crashes, or if it does, it's only for other, inferior drivers. The result? I, and maybe I alone, can speed.

In reality, of course, speeding is a risky driving behavior and it will cause crashes. I may come to a false positive conclusion that the relationship between speeding and crashing does not exist for me. This may result in my becoming an over-confident driver. I now have a sense of superiority and invincibility, and I am an incident waiting to happen. You and I will finally see it once my luck runs out and I finally become a statistic in the thirty instances of ties we discussed earlier.

If there is a ten to fifteen relationship between risky driving behaviors and hard-evidenced results, such as crashes and fatalities, then there are 290 to 435 risky driving behaviors to observe before a tie results in those twenty-nine incidents and the one fatality. That means that with 43,000 fatalities, there are up to 18,705,000 clues to predict and prevent the devastation and destruction in the United States alone.

With a Driver Risk Management Program, it's easy to observe the risky driving behaviors in thousands of drivers in thousands of vehicles. Unlike the disadvantage under which everyone else operates, I've seen the behaviors that are exposing the driver and his company to undue risk and certain future expense, simply because these are the precursors to the death and destruction that everyone else sees only after the fact.

Unfortunately, that's when the proverbial horse is already out of the barn and the tragedy of the tie has enacted its toll.

The encouraging and exciting part about all of this, however, is that since we can observe risky behaviors before they result in the awful consequences, we can intervene in the process and reduce or eliminate risky driving behaviors using a Driver Risk Management Program. And we can eliminate the crashes. Along with the death, destruction and costs that accompany them.

Something amazing happens when a driver knows that his or her risky driving behavior will be measured and coached. What's even more amazing is what happens when a driver realizes that bad driving behavior actually matters before the crash happens. The result is a quick adjustment in their driving habits to avoid the consequence of a coach reviewing an audio-video clip of their actual driving behavior.

## PRIMARY SAFE DRIVING SKILLS

These are some of the primary safe driving skills that are key to success behind the wheel. The lack of one or more of these fundamentals is often an important ingredient in an audio-video review clip.

### Proper Seeing Skills
- Look 15 seconds ahead
- Scan from sidewalk to sidewalk (or more)
- Check mirrors frequently
- Look left-right-left at intersections
- Don't fixate

### Indicators of Poor Seeing Skills
- Late, hard braking
- Swerving
- No adjustment to others' erratic actions
- Poor decision-making
- Getting boxed in
- Collision

### Proper Space Management
- Proper following distance
- Avoiding the herd mentality
- Prudent lane selection
- Adequate space in front when stopped

### Indicators of Poor Space Management
- Frequent hard braking
- Inadequate following distance
- Traveling in clusters
- Abrupt evasive actions
- Poor decision-making
- Collision

### Other Driving-Related Issues
- Speeding
- Use of a cell phone when driving
- Reading, eating and other forms of inattention
- No seatbelt use
- Lack of care for the vehicle
- Rage and other emotional outbursts

Coaching works. This reviewing process produces several tangible results without fail. And, it reduces the frequency of risky driving instances by 50 percent. Amazingly, it's been proven to reduce the frequency of risky driving in teenagers by 70 percent! In addition, it reduces the severity of the actual incidents by an even greater extent, and it protects and exonerates the driver from fraud or others' risky maneuvers or even from himself. Ultimately, when you see what you were actually doing on an audio-video review clip and understand the behavior that needs to change in order to protect you from risk, you adjust your behavior substantially and immediately. Risk scores now become more than just numbers on a piece of paper.

As a result, your risk score is the most salient predictor of if, whether and when you will become a statistic. When you can predict it, you can prevent it, and that saves lives and dollars. You can take that to the bank!

---

[1] Insurance Institute for Highway Safety. Fatality Facts: Teenagers. Available: http://www.iihs.org/research/fatality_facts_2006/teenagers.html Accessed January 24, 2008.

[2] National Highway Traffic Safety Administration. Traffic Safety Facts: Young Drivers. Available: http://www-nrd.nhtsa.dot.gov/Pubs/810817. PDF Accessed January 24, 2008.

[3] Department of Health and Human Services, Centers for Disease Control and Prevention

## Chapter 5

# 100 Years of Driving and Still Living in the Dark Ages

Sometimes I feel as though we are living in the Dark Ages. In fact, when future generations look back upon our time here on Earth, I know they will conclude that we were.

In my working lifetime, I have seen the transition from being accosted by second-hand smoke in meeting rooms to now seeing a ban on smoking for an entire city in California. Not to mention a ban on smoking in the pubs of merry old England. I've seen the emergence of seat belts and air bags to their mandatory inclusion in all passenger vehicles. And, I'm watching cell phones slowly (too slowly to my way of thinking) disappear from the hands of drivers on a state-by-state basis.

Once society decides to take action against harmful or inane practices, it is easy to look back in wonderment at how we ever tolerated a particular system in the first place. Getting change to occur on a mass scale is always frustrating and painfully slow no matter how compelling the change, nor how ridiculous the incumbent methodology. Unfortunately, the wheels of progress move slowly.

It seems obvious now that the automobile was going to all but eliminate the horse as a viable method of transporting humans and goods, but I also know there were several excellent buggy-whip companies who hung in there until the last hoof clopped, waiting for something like $100/barrel crude oil prices to ruin the whole system; as if that would ever happen!

At some point, though, as more and more steering wheels replaced more and more horseshoes, this new-fangled phenomenon began causing other societal woes.

These Iron Horses required roads, gas stations, drive-in restaurants and motels. The more mobile people became, the more demand was created for goods and services that only a few short decades before could not even be envisioned. And, along with these economic benefits and new-found freedoms came costs and regulations. Yes, every yin has its yang.

## Who Can Be Trusted?

As the Iron Horse became ubiquitous, it quickly became apparent that we couldn't just let people buy an automobile, allow them to go out onto the public thoroughfares and run right into one another. There were rules and regulations to make and enforce, along with taxes to be levied. And, if in doing so the politicians generated revenue for the state, it couldn't be all that bad now, could it?

So they quickly began to grasp the American Dream. If we can regulate it and tax it, then we can make it better. It's the governmental version of "If you build it, they will come," except that it is embodied more in a sentiment of "If we tax it, they must pay it." This led to some bright individual coming up with this gem:

> "I know, we'll make them earn and pay for a driver's license! It will be done state by state, and each state will have its own rules of the road. We will teach and train people how to drive and to share our common infrastructures. We will indoctrinate them thoroughly when they are sixteen years old. Then, we'll make them prove that they've learned both how to operate a motor vehicle and also how to operate the vehicle on our state highways and city streets."

"Well, that sounds right. But how will we know that they are up to the standards that would confer upon them this state driver's license of which you dream?"

"I know this is getting kinda difficult, so stay with me here on this one. We make them take a written examination and then they have to go out with a state driver's license employee sitting right next to them and prove they can do it!"

"Right in front of him? Right there in the passenger seat watching every move he makes with a clipboard in his lap?"

"Once! Then, and this is the best part from a revenue generating standpoint, if a law enforcement official of any kind, observes a licensed driver breaking any of the rules of the road, they can be issued a ticket!"

"Oh man! This is too good! A ticket will cost them money and penalize them for not driving the exact same way they drove when we issued them their state-certified license on that day when they were sixteen."

"Right, so we teach them the right things to do when they are sixteen. Then we turn them loose to behave in any manner they see fit. But we hope they remember the rules and obey them. But, if they don't and we catch them, we charge them a fine for misbehaving."

"Man, that's genius!"

No, that's the Dark Ages. Can you imagine this system working in almost any other situation? Consider this …

"Kids, your Dad and I are going on a two-week cruise to Alaska and it's the long-overdue, belated honeymoon we never got to take before you were born. This is important to us and we trust you. We know you are sixteen and seventeen and you know the rules. No parties, no kids in the house, no drinking, feed the dog, change the cat litter, water the plants and get to bed by midnight every night.

"Now, we're not going to have anyone check in on you or even call you ourselves because you know what we expect and you know what to do. So, unless we get a police report or the neighbors call us to complain, we have every confidence that you will behave and perform as though we are here to observe you ourselves."

If your mind isn't instantly flashing back to Tom Cruise dancing in his skivvies playing the air guitar in *Risky Business*, you haven't seen the movie.

But I digress. For those of you culturally challenged individuals who have not seen Tom as the enterprising young Joel Goodsen in this 1983 classic, he does end up depositing his dad's Porsche into Lake Michigan in between running a brothel out of his parent's upscale home in their North Shore Chicago suburban neighborhood. All in a weekend.

But, before you leap to concluding that it is those teenage hormones that are the root cause of all risky behavior or misplaced trust, think again. Think about deploying the "Train Me Once and Trust I'll Behave Unless, and Until, You Catch Me Doing Otherwise" concept in any other endeavor you may undertake in life. Goodbye to those long security lines at the airport! Simply tell the passengers what can't be brought aboard and, *voilà*—those pesky strip searches are now a thing of the past. **Right?**

Or IRS audits? Forgetaboutit! We all know that everyone wants to be honest and carry his or her fair share of the load. **Right?**

Say goodbye to the radar detector industry. No need any longer because we won't have police cars hiding in concealed places to trap unsuspecting motorists with a radar gun to prove they were going over the speed limit. Once we actually tell them, teach them and certify them as qualified drivers, they simply won't speed. **Right?**

## Wrong. Wrong. Wrong.

Unfortunately, we've learned that just training, telling and certifying someone to do a particular task doesn't mean we can rely on his good will and character to carry the day for us.

Human behavior simply doesn't work that way. We learn more from the consequences of our actions than we do from someone else telling us what those consequences will be.

> Of course, we all behaved impeccably when we were sixteen and desperate to obtain our driver's license while our new best friend was sitting in the passenger seat observing everything we did and scribbling our fate on that clipboard.

> Of course, we all know what the legal speed limit is and also that we should not exceed it.

> Of course, we all know not to tail gate, get boxed in or drive with our knees while eating a sandwich.

> And, of course, we all know that we should be scanning our mirrors and looking ahead instead of turning all the way around to glare at our unruly kids in the back of our mini-vans.

But, do these obvious safety regulations keep us from doing what we shouldn't? We do it because we think we can. Either we have always gotten away with it before, or we've become over-confident in our driving skills and abilities.

That's why I can only anticipate the day when we realize the ridiculous folly of following an archaic system where we test and verify once and then trust that humans will run counter to their very nature and do what we ask, instead of what they can. Consider that our current system of driver licenses was created back in 1910 and we're still using the same system today—nearly 100 years later!

France and Germany were among the earliest countries to require mandatory driver licensing, right at the start of the twentieth century. As automobile-related fatalities soared in North America, public outcry provoked legislators to begin studying the French and German statutes as models. On August 1, 1910, North America's first driver licensing law went into effect in the state of New York, though it initially applied only to professional chauffeurs. In July of 1913, the state of New Jersey became the first to require *all* drivers to pass a mandatory examination before receiving a license.

In the United States, the driving age is determined by each state or territory, with the most common age being sixteen. The minimum age for a license varies from fourteen years three months to eighteen years. Most states and territories also have learner driver's licenses (also called learner's permit), which allow a person to drive, provided they are accompanied by a licensed driver. Learner's permits are granted by some states to drivers as young as fourteen.

In the past decade, fewer and fewer teenagers obtained driver's licenses. According to a December 2, 2004 *Los Angeles Times* article, only 43 percent of American sixteen- and seventeen-year-olds had licenses in 2002. By comparison, the percentage in 1982 was 52 percent. The rate is even lower in some states (e.g., 9 percent in Missouri). The decrease in percentages are said to be due to the many restrictions that an average teen must face overall in order to obtain the licenses. Instead of facing these provisions, many drivers under the age of eighteen today simply wait until they turn eighteen to get their driver's license.

## Change on the Horizon

Many states have changed the rules for new drivers, especially the guidelines that are for teenagers under the age of eighteen. These new drivers cannot go straight from a learner's permit to a full valid license. Instead, these new drivers are required to go through a graduated licensing system that includes at least one more step and many more rules and restrictions.

New teenage drivers might be unhappy with these new licensing systems in various states, but the changes were made to make these new drivers better drivers. New teenage drivers are typically not as mature as most drivers currently on the roadways, and they definitely do not have the driving experience of other motorists. As a result of immaturity and limited driving skills, teens are more at risk to have a collision.

Graduated driver licensing (GDL) is a system of laws and practices that gradually introduces young drivers into the driving population.

This is typically done by imposing an intermediate or provisional license in between the learner permit and full valid license. The GDL is able to cut down on collisions and fatal crashes by prolonging the learning process for young novice drivers. The purpose of the GDL program is to allow young drivers to safely garner driving experience, and hopefully a bit of maturity, before obtaining full driving privileges in their state. The GDL is typically targeted at teenagers, thus those young drivers under the age of eighteen. Depending on the state's driving laws, the first step can be started at fourteen, fifteen or sixteen.

The terms of a GDL program will vary depending on the state laws, but generally most states require in the first step having a learner's permit, and an over-twenty-one adult with a valid driver's license, which they have had for a certain number of years, present in the front seat while the new young driver is operating the motor vehicle. The teen then must take a certified driver education course while holding her learner's permit for a period of three to six months. After these stipulations have been met, the driver can take the next step and take the driving test. After passing the driving test, the provisional or intermediate license is the next step of the graduated licensing system.

As the graduating system implies, the person has graduated to a new level at this point so some restrictions are taken away, but they are not yet fully licensed without any restrictions. Again, the provisions for an intermediate license will differ according to state laws, but basically at this stage the teen can drive during daylight hours without an adult, but are required to have one during late night hours, or are not allowed to do night-time driving at all. They are restricted to the number of passengers they can have, have supervised practice sessions, and are not allowed to have alcohol in their vehicle at any time.

To obtain a full license, the driver must have completed both stages one and two of the graduated licensing process. The provisional license typically must be held for a period of six, eight or twelve months, and the driver must be of a minimum age before he can apply for a full state license. Many states require that the person also not have received any traffic violations before acquiring his full license, or they will have to wait to apply for it.

It's hard to believe that nearly 100 years since driver's licensing began, the system really has not changed. However, when the day for change comes, we may indeed have a system that takes risk out of driving by observing how people actually behave, instead of how we wish they would comport themselves in an ideal world. In that new age, driver observations will allow consequences to drive behavior before we, or someone we love, become another expensive statistic.

Until then, we continue to live in the Dark Ages.

However, once we confront reality and emerge from the Dark Ages, we can essentially have that same level of devotion to rules and safety that we all once had on that one testing day when we were sixteen and had to perform flawlessly for our clipboard buddy.

As the old saying goes, you get what you inspect, not what you expect.

That's why exception-based video event recorders are now becoming more prevalent in fleets and automobiles. Drivers need to know what they're doing wrong so they can correct it. People develop habits they don't even know they have. It's like listening to your voice on a tape recorder. "That can't be me!" When you see your actions on a video, the first reaction is, "I didn't do that." It's hard, however, to argue with what you see on tape.

This is one area where emerging from those Dark Ages can positively impact lives and money, and society can benefit.

## Chapter 6

# That Work/Life Balance Takes a Helluva Commute

Fuel costs are rising to unprecedented levels, health care is unaffordable for a huge proportion of the country, hours of work are getting longer and the pressure to compete efficiently in a world economy requires fewer people to do more for less.

Never before in man's history have we had so much technology, tools and entertainment at our disposal with so very little time to make use of or enjoy it. I remember when everyone was touting the advent of computers to help make life easier and help us create a paperless society. CBS Radio syndicated columnist David Ross captured the essence of a paperless society best when he said, "The best thing about the Internet is that there's no paper. The worst thing about the Internet is that there's no paper. Thousands of organizations are now using the World Wide Web and office Intranets to distribute information, much of which winds up being printed by the recipient."

Who would have thought that such a liberating concept as working virtually would result in essentially feeling enslaved and on-call 24/7, every week of the year, including throughout vacation? No wonder BlackBerry users are now called "CrackBerrys." BlackBerry devices and other smart phones may have had a huge impact on executive and employee productivity, but they also have had a negative impact on work-life balance by making it more difficult to switch off from the office, according to a recent survey. The study, conducted by BlackBerry maker Research In Motion, found that an average BlackBerry user converts one hour of downtime to productive time each day, and increases overall team efficiency by 38 percent.

"Improvement in productivity has been huge—the ability to respond immediately has been a real bonus for the company," said Kevin Fitzpatrick, chief information officer at food services provider Sodexho's U.K. operations. "Work-life balance swings dramatically to the company side of the scales." You may not have to be physically in a particular location for specific blocks of time every Monday through Friday like your mother and father did, but you have to be mentally engaged almost every waking moment—IF you can sleep at all.

There's no escape. We have cell phones to make use of those pesky moments when we are trying to board an airplane. What used to be a quiet time to reflect upon our upcoming adventure or look at the in-flight magazine after loading our luggage is no more. What used to be an opportunity to converse (do people converse anymore?) with the person sitting in the middle seat, trying to impress them with our superior business knowledge, our children or grandchildren, our busy meeting schedule or … you fill in the blank for the best method of power positioning … is now a time to stay connected for just one more minute. Can you imagine what it will be like once the airlines allow us to continue our conversations throughout the entire flight? And you thought crying babies impinged on your sanctity of peace and quiet.

By either text messaging or e-mailing one last thing, we can stay connected with our own little world before we are forced to shut down our little electronic ankle bracelets. And if that's not enough, we can be bombarded by headline news while shaving so we are spared the turmoil and trauma of having to ferret out who is saying what to advance which agenda for whose benefit.

Yeah, I'm just as guilty as the next guy. As *Inc.* magazine recently reported in an exclusive interview concerning my individual work habits …

*The first thing I do when I get up—before I even go to the restroom or anything—I'll grab my BlackBerry and see what the issues are. Then I'll take it with me to the bathroom and go through all my e-mails. I get 80 or 100 a day, and I have to know what's okay or what isn't okay. Then I'll brush my teeth and take a shower. Some mornings it's a struggle to get dressed before you're writing back different e-mails on the BlackBerry.*

*I get to work about 7:30. I've had to really force myself not to read the BlackBerry while I'm driving, though I don't always even succeed at that. And I'm the guy that's supposed to be about driver safety. When I get in, I put my PC, which I've brought from home, into the docking station. I'm compulsive about my e-mail. That's my primary communication with the rest of the enterprise. It's a one-to-many communication so it's more efficient.*

I'm not proud of it, but it's what I've become. Yes, I've joined the mass of humanity trying to make the most of every waking moment.

How many people still engage in that quaint tradition of grocery shopping in order to prepare a meal when eating out is surely cheaper and faster? Our technological society allows us to easily escape those awkward moments awaiting checkout by staying focused upon the plasma screen in front of us. Courtesy of the latest communication technology, we no longer have to worry about losing track of which country Angelina will adopt from next or how the Olsen twins are keeping those unsightly pounds off. Now, thankfully, our minds need not be cluttered with thoughts during the actual checkout process because we can scan, weigh and bag our own stuff with technology that is so cool that we have liberated those poor cashiers from a life of standing on their feet all day in a dead-end job in an actual physical location!

Why learn to hit a golf ball when you can hit farther and more accurately with the click of a mouse? Hitting a 95 mph fastball becomes a cinch. When it's virtual.

I can watch almost any movie, almost anytime, on almost any device, almost anywhere. It may only be 3" square, but I'm still living in the moment. How many of you are like me—old enough to remember when it was a very special event to watch *The Wizard of Oz* or *Miracle on 34th Street*, once a year in the season? That one special time when the family would gather around the one black-and-white television with hot chocolate and savor the moment and create a memory that would last a lifetime. Now I can resurrect Elvis live anytime, anywhere without even going to Vegas!

As is true with almost everything in life, too much of a good thing can be detrimental, or good things done in excess can be harmful or fatal. What I am describing here is a case of …

## Compulsion, Abuse and Betrayal

To allow ourselves to become slaves to the very tools we invented to serve us as their masters is a compulsion. With the possible exception of doctors and drug dealers, there is no compelling reason to stay in constant 24/7 communications with the office or the customer. It is compulsion and a fear of being out of the loop, out of control and out of touch.

There are exceptions to every rule, of course, and there are legitimate times. Take, for instance, when your wife is in labor and you are in the car racing to the hospital to meet her. You haven't done the ultrasound and you're naturally curious as to which color to paint the bedroom. Answer the phone! But in general, you don't need to answer every cell phone, text message or e-mail message every minute of every day. At least not while you're driving!

We abuse technology so much that it is our own quality of life that suffers. Perpetual mental motion impedes our body's ability to rest, restore and recuperate. We are stressed out, fatigued and emotionally drained from the relentless call to be on call and be productive nearly every minute of every day.

I was recently at a Los Angeles Angel's baseball game and couldn't help but notice the number of people incessantly on their cell phones and BlackBerrys, even among the loud cheering and constant action. The Angels beat the Tigers 11 to 4, if memory serves, so it's not like a no-action game got people to seek other diversions. They simply couldn't pull themselves away from something as urgent as what sale a colleague might have closed or, even more importantly, the reminder to pick up milk on the way home.

We order food online, pay bills online and shop for everything from clothes to insurance online. We have even resorted to searching for our soul mates online. Of course, the Internet has long been a source for short-term dating and vicarious stimulation of all types and natures. But, we won't drag ourselves down that hole at this time.

The inescapable irony is that we have invented, and are perfecting, a virtual world that obviates the need for actual interaction in many circumstances. The freedom to work, shop, game, date, gamble, bank, and practically any other verb, virtually erodes our natural skills and abilities, if not our drive, to do so physically, literally and actually. So as in any endeavor, the better one becomes virtually is achieved at the expense of the actual or physical activity. Therein lays the abuse of technology.

The betrayal then is to our own physical nature and health. As we further entrench in the full-time access and demands of the virtual world our technology has enabled, we are betraying the organic and natural essence of what it is to be human and what got us to where and who we are. Even now, life extension is possible through artificial hearts and limbs. One can easily see various enhancements to the brain, as well as the brawn.

The dichotomy between the natural and physical worlds is stark enough, and they are blending and blurring faster than most of us are comfortable with. However, it is when we force their combining by trying to live in each separate world simultaneously, and without a rational blending, that we quickly get into very dangerous territory.

It is one thing to have an artificial heart or augmented breasts, going about our normal work and recreational lives being somewhat bionic in a physical world. But it is quite another to be mentally in a virtual or fantasy world while operating and interacting in the physical world.

Most of us would not be keen to face a real Roger Clemens' fastball after hitting a fantasy home run off of his image in an Xbox® game. We keep perspective on what is real and what is fantasy, or at least what is virtual reality.

But, there are dangerous areas of intersection between reality and technology where the lines do not, and should not, blur. These lines, which we insist on crossing defiantly do not co-exist well. One of them is when we are driving.

Where power steering and even navigation technology have enhanced and improved the driving experience, text messaging and cell phone usage while driving can have fatal consequences. We have grown accustomed to multi-tasking and being in touch with all constituents at all times. Where technology has blended into the vehicle or into the human, the result can be positive and additive. Where the two remain distinct and separate, but engaged simultaneously, the result is risky and dangerous, at best, and fatal all too often.

## Beyond Abuse

Take cell phones ... please! This ubiquitous communication device has grown beyond what could only have been imagined just a few short years ago. If only Dick Tracy were here today. As we discussed before, everything has its yin and yang. Good and bad. Pro and con. For cell phones, the yang, bad and con is the way they are used—and abused—while driving.

In the United States, over 236 million people subscribed to cell phones as of May 2007, compared with approximately 4.3 million in 1990, according to the Cellular Telecommunications & Internet Association. Consider this: That's nearly one cell phone for each man, woman and child. Let's take this one step further. As of the end of 2006, there were about 2.5 billion cell phones on active accounts in the world. Somewhere on the order of another half a billion are going to be added in 2007, and again in 2008, for a total of 3.5 billion. Guess what? That's more than half of the people in the world.[1]

It's a well-known fact that increased reliance on cell phones has led to a rise in the number of people who use the devices while driving. There are two dangers associated with driving and cell-phone use. First, drivers must take their eyes off the road while dialing. Second, people can become so absorbed in their conversations that their ability to concentrate on the act of driving is severely impaired, jeopardizing the safety of vehicle occupants and pedestrians. Since the first law was passed in New York in 2001 banning hand-held cell-phone use while driving, there has been debate as to the exact nature and degree of the hazard. The latest research shows that while using a cell phone when driving may not be the most dangerous distraction, it is by far the most common cause of vehicle crashes and near-crashes due to its prevalence.

A survey of dangerous driver behavior was released in January 2007 by Nationwide Mutual Insurance Co. The survey of 1,200 drivers found that 73 percent talk on cell phones while driving. Not surprisingly, cell phone use was highest among young drivers.

Text messaging, or "texting" by teens, a driving distraction related to cell phone use, was the subject of an August 2006 *Teens Today* survey conducted by the Liberty Mutual Research Institute for Safety and Students Against Destructive Decisions (SADD). The survey showed that teens considered sending text messages via cell phones to be their biggest distraction. Of the teens surveyed, 37 percent said that text messaging was extremely or very distracting, while 20 percent said that they were distracted by their emotional states. In addition, 19 percent said that having friends in the car was distracting. The January 2007 survey by the insurer Nationwide found that 19 percent of motorists say they text message while driving.

A study released in April 2006 found that almost 80 percent of crashes and 65 percent of near-crashes involved some form of driver inattention within three seconds of the event. The study, *The 100-Car Naturalistic Driving Study*, conducted by the Virginia Tech Transportation Institute and the National Highway Traffic Safety Administration (NHTSA), breaks new ground. (Earlier research found that driver inattention was responsible for 25 to 30 percent of crashes.) The new study found that the most common distraction is the use of cell phones.

## Is Hands-Free Actually Better?

Motorists who use cell phones while driving are *four times* as likely to get into crashes serious enough to injure themselves, according to a study of drivers in Perth, Australia, conducted by the Insurance Institute for Highway Safety. The results, published in July 2005, suggest that banning hand-held phone use won't necessarily improve safety if drivers simply switch to hands-free phones. The study found that injury crash risk didn't vary with type of phone.[2]

Many studies have shown that using hand-held cell phones while driving can constitute a hazardous distraction. However, the theory that hands-free sets are safer has been challenged by the findings of several studies. A study from researchers at the University of Utah, published in the summer 2006 issue of *Human Factors*, the quarterly journal of the Human Factors and Ergonomics Society, concludes that talking on a cell phone while driving is as dangerous as driving drunk, even if the phone is a hands-free model. An earlier study by researchers at the university found that motorists who talked on hands-free cell phones were 18 percent slower in braking and took 17 percent longer to regain the speed they lost when they braked.

As many as forty countries may restrict or prohibit the use of cell phones while driving. In fact, most countries prohibit the use of hand-held phones while driving. Supporters of restrictions on driving while using a cell phone say that the distractions associated with cell phone use while driving are far greater than other distractions. Conversations using a cell phone demand greater continuous concentration, which diverts the driver's eyes from the road and his mind from driving.[3]

It is difficult enough to cope with all of the rapid technological advancements and demands forever increasing productivity and efficiency, while continuing to maintain some modicum of humanity. The lines continue to blur and the boundaries between the two get pressured continuously. To multi-task or mix the use of technology to do anything other than focus more on the task at hand, while driving, is irresponsible and potentially lethal.

We live in an outrageously fortunate and prosperous time. We are the most productive people in the history of the planet. We may contemplate, as Hamlet once did, whether 'tis nobler to suffer the slings and arrows of outrageous fortune, but to do so while text messaging the concept as we are driving is to play Russian roulette at the wheel.

To be or not to be, should not be the question.

---

[1] Michael S. Hart, Founder of Project Gutenberg, Inventor of eBook Libraries

[2] McEvoy SP; Stevenson MR; McCartt AT; Woodward M; Haworth C; Palamara P; Cercarelli R. 2005. Role of mobile phones in motor vehicle crashes resulting in hospital attendance: a case-crossover study. British Medical Journal 331: 428–430.

[3] Insurance Information Institute, October 2007

## Chapter 7

# Remember Your First Time?

Back to the dream music and time machine. Once upon a time …

There was a nice, wholesome middle-class family growing up in suburbia with all of the modern conveniences—a television, a telephone and long-play records. Televangelists and telemarketers were as yet unhatched.

Ward dutifully went to work each morning to his stable, though non-descript, job while June cheerfully greeted him at the door each evening upon his return. Ward knew that job could last his entire career if he could evade any major social faux pas with his boss. Their sons, Wally and Theodore (yes, "The Beaver") went to school, played sports and progressed through various maturation phases. Nobody got suspended for texting during class, and no one got shot at their schools, unless you count Eddie scoring a direct hit on Lumpy with a spitball.

This was a more even-paced, almost sedated lifestyle compared to today's standards.

Before the advent of the Internet, satellite phones and cable television, life had a pace that was measured in years, if not generations, and certain rights of passage came along at a comparative turtle's pace to today's rabbit.

One such long-anticipated and excruciatingly slow right of passage was testing for, and getting, your driver's license. This was the subject of much anxiety and folklore at my school. I'm sure it was at yours, as well.

The driving test in-vehicle evaluators (the "testers") were mean and unreasonable. Some of them would flunk you on your first try no matter what you did. Of course, you thought that if you were respectful and friendly this would give you an edge. Or it wouldn't because they would think you were trying to charm your way through the test. Each of us had our own ways of trying to beat the system. No matter how hard we tried, none of them seemed to work.

Is your heart rate rising as you relive this distant memory? If not, then this next memory jog will definitely get your pulse racing. Remember parallel parking? It was the most intimidating and daunting of all the potential areas for failing. It occupied most of our mental energy, rightfully so. The strategy of how, if or on what number of tries you would pass the driving test for your coveted license to freedom was the subject of many teenage dreams, fantasies and nightmares.

If only self-parking cars were available when we were taking our tests. Self-parking, you ask? Yes, technology now has an answer—cars that park themselves. Imagine finding the perfect parking spot, but instead of struggling to maneuver your car back and forth, you simply press a button, sit back and relax. Self-parking cars currently on the market are not completely autonomous, but they do make parallel parking much easier. The driver still regulates the speed of the vehicle by pressing and releasing the brake pedal (the car's idle speed is enough to move it into the parking space without pressing the gas pedal). Once the process begins, the on-board computer system takes over the steering wheel. *Voilà!*

## That Fateful Day

When I think back to my own fateful day, I remember it as a cold snowy January in Chicago. (Is there any other kind?) My poor father, who had lost his own license due to drunk driving, had to impose upon a licensed friend to drive me to take the test in the near-blizzard conditions.

To say I was strong-willed and on a mission would be an understatement. I bet my parents' private observations at the time would have included incendiary phrases like demanding, manipulative, unreasonable and domineering. Who knew these very descriptors would be found, decades later, in my own job description?

As I nervously settled into my father's friend's unfamiliar car to take the long-awaited test, I tried to size up the cold, humorless enigma—clipboard in hand—who was buckling into the passenger's seat next to me. I checked the mirrors. I buckled the seat belt. I started the engine. I made full and complete stops. I even looked both ways. I did everything exactly by the book. In fact, it strikes me now that that was probably the last time I ever behaved exactly that way, when the man with the cold stare and the clipboard sat next to me evaluating everything I did, and didn't do, that fateful snowy day.

In the slower paced pre-Internet days of longer, safer business and life cycles, we took that test. It was also a time when we might have had to actually go through that driving road test another time when our license was up for renewal, or if we had received too many traffic violations in the interim.

## Life after the Driver's Test

But, as technology progresses, so does our ability to efficiently and practically train or re-train. In the commercial world, professional fleet drivers can go through training once a year, or even monthly, using the Internet or e-learning. With the new technology, we can test and verify safe driving practices in addition to basic training. Anywhere. Anytime. Now that's progress!

This is a vast improvement over the once- or twice-in-a-lifetime event of sitting next to the Good Humor Man with the clipboard. However, it is still far short of actually getting grown-up, trained, licensed drivers to drive safely and responsibly like they did the first day they ever got their license. The reason for that gap between performance and expectation is, of course, that you get what you inspect, not what you expect. Ronald Reagan once famously said, "Trust … and verify."

The next obvious step in using technology for ever-faster communications and results is to get observations of each of us driving, but only when we actually perform in some risky or potentially unsafe manner.

Instead of training based upon some pre-set time increments, such as yearly or monthly, and then training all aspects of driving to all people, Driver Risk Management (DRM) programs with exception-based video event recorders provide a real-time, Internet-based observation system that only focuses on which driver needs what training or reinforcement, and only when they need that feedback.

If, for example, I start to drift into a habit of following too closely, or not checking my mirrors, and as a result, I have to swerve or slam on the brakes, it's obvious that I had not appropriately anticipated what I might have to do with my car's direction and velocity. The result is that I reacted to the new stimuli by dodging the proverbial bullet. Dodging is a risky driving maneuver. Luck is another.

With a DRM program, I can receive the real-time observation and subsequent coaching or training I need, but only if I really need it and only about what I specifically need. The best part is that it's delivered quickly and efficiently so I can get back to what I do best—driving.

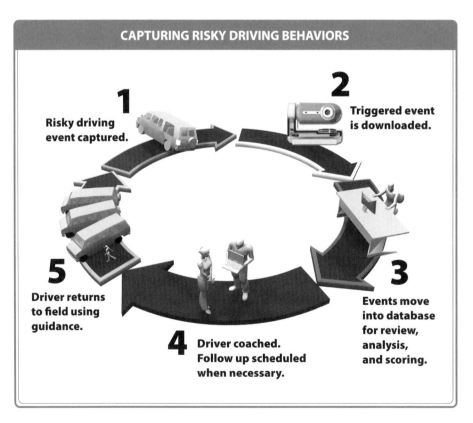

**CAPTURING RISKY DRIVING BEHAVIORS**

**1** Risky driving event captured.

**2** Triggered event is downloaded.

**3** Events move into database for review, analysis, and scoring.

**4** Driver coached. Follow up scheduled when necessary.

**5** Driver returns to field using guidance.

## DRIVER RISK MANAGEMENT REPORT CARD

**NAME:**   John Doe
**DATE:**   December 13, 2007

### ROOT CAUSES:

| | |
|---|---|
| Cell Phone | ✔ **Mapping/Navigation** |
| Food or Drink | Passenger |
| Not Looking Far Ahead | Blank Stare |
| ✔ **Not Scanning Roadway** | Intersection Not Scanned |
| Mirrors Not Checked | Blind Area Not Checked |
| Judgment Error | Somewhat Aggressive |
| Aggressive | Willful Misconduct |
| Drowsy/Falling Asleep | Driver Unbelted |
| Passenger Unbelted | Following Too Close |
| Unsafe Speed | Traffic Violation |
| Failed to Keep an Out | Poor Lane Selection |
| In Other's Blind Area | |

**Comments:** John's driving has improved and he has become a safer driver. He no longer talks on his cell phone and now wears his seatbelt each time he sits down.

**Improvements Recommended:** Be sure to keep a safe distance and scan ahead.

## The Power of False-Positive Reinforcement

We humans all behave based upon what we expect to happen as a result of our actions. Think about your own behavior: If I do this, I will likely get that. For instance, if I answer "yes" to my wife's rhetorical question of "Does this make me look fat?" I can expect to sleep in another room that night.

In driving, we also get reinforced by what we anticipate will happen when we behave in a certain way. If I have always tailgated and I never hit anything, I am getting positive reinforcement that I can actually perform this risky act flawlessly, again and again. Basically, it has never cost me before, therefore I can continue doing it. I've learned that I have greater vision, reflexes and anticipation than mere mortal humans.

Ironically, that continual loop of what I call "false-positive rein-forcement" leads to over-confidence. In reality, this is a collision waiting to happen. The only difference between your tailgating successfully the thousands of times you got away with it before and the one time you will not get away with it this time is luck. Sound familiar? This is simply pure unadulterated luck because this time, two physical objects did not attempt to occupy the exact same physical space at the exact same time. If they had, you wouldn't have been as lucky. Or blessed with good fortune.

Keep in mind that the risky behavior still occurred, but luck was the variable. With a video event recorder in the vehicle, we can "see" the accident before it actually happens, before the luck runs out. We can draw the driver's attention to the behavior that the Good Humor Man with the clipboard would have flunked him for. And we can help him improve his driving, save lives and help our bottom line.

## Did I or Didn't I?

By the way, I did pass my driver's test that snowy January day in Chicago so many years ago on my very first try. Wanna know why?

Essentially, it was a lack of perspective and my good life-long buddy, named "Luck."

After trying so hard to do everything perfectly during my driver's test, I felt I had blown it on the parallel parking part. So I was angry and disappointed with myself. I decided that since I had nothing else to lose for the remainder of the test, I would just relax and drive naturally without worrying about anything that might be written on the clipboard. That renewed self-confidence translated to the tester judging that I was a confident and capable person able to control my vehicle properly.

ZITS © ZITS PARTNERSHIP, KING FEATURES SYNDICATE

Luck and a lack of proper perspective got me to this point. But I'm getting too old and too wise to continue pressing my luck. Maybe it's time for a new buddy.

### Making Your First Time Every Time

Our driver's test is a once-in-a-lifetime experience. But, what if our Clipboard Buddy were able to ride along with us everyday? Watching, recording and reporting on what we did and how we did it? Think about how much better our driving would be. That's exactly what a DRM program does. By using exception-based video event recorders, this real-time, Internet-based observation system focuses on which drivers need what kind of training. But, the key to a successful program is the way it is implemented. Here are a few key tips to ensure that a DRM program is easily implemented into your safety program:

- **Get all your stakeholders on board.**
Meet internally with everyone involved so they understand what the DRM solution entails and what each individual's role will be in executing the program. Be sure to set guidelines on how quickly incidents should be coached and how/where to provide that coaching.

- **Communicate with your drivers.**
Host an orientation to explain to drivers why the company is implementing a DRM solution and what benefits the drivers will receive from the solution. Be sure to introduce the DRM solution to your drivers before they ever see a video event recorder in their vehicles so they know what to expect. This would be a good opportunity to bring in your human resources department, who should have already been brought on board with the program. Finally, have all of your employees sign a form acknowledging that they were educated on the DRM solution.

- **Deploy the solution in both driver and manager vehicles.**
This will send the message that implementing the DRM solution is not about an individual driver; it is about making the organization safer as a whole.

- **Implement a rewards system.**
The DRM solution is exception based and will only be triggered by force making it difficult to capture when drivers are exhibiting good driving behavior. One way to

identify good behavior is by measuring the time or distance the driver goes without triggering the solution. Create a program that rewards drivers in these situations and recognizes them when they have reached a designated milestone. Offering rewards to drivers reinforces the need to eliminate risky driving behaviors.

- **Continual communication.**
  DRM programs are most successful when continual communication is present. Show a meaningful driving clip at safety meetings, circulate reports to upper management or include a column about the solution in every newsletter—just be sure to keep the flow of communication open and moving.

- **Success hinges on local people actually deploying and managing the program.**
  Be sure that each manager has specific objectives and the financial incentive to achieve their objectives. Focus on improving risky behavior, not on reducing collisions, and look at leading indicators—risk—not lagging indicators—collisions.

- **Use the solution as a tool to report near collisions, in order to foster discussion on improving risky driving behaviors.**
  Many companies ask that drivers report near collisions, but few drivers do. With a DRM solution, the video event recorder will, most likely, capture the near collision and open the forum for the driver and supervisor to discuss what happened and how the risky behavior involved could be eliminated. Use this captured near collision as a training tool. Secure permission from the driver, or only use the front view, and show the video at a safety meeting as an example of a common mistake that everyone makes and how to learn from it.

- **Create and communicate the ground rules of the program.**
  Determine in advance of roll-out how you plan to handle most situations identified by DriveCam footage. For example, what behaviors will constitute the need for coaching? Establish the plan and then communicate it to your drivers. Drivers will work hard to comply once they understand the ground rules.

- **Provide positive and consistent coaching.**
  One of the most important aspects of a successful DRM implementation is how coaching and feedback are handled—only by receiving appropriate feedback is a driver's behavior going to improve. One example is finding a reasonably private area in which to hold the coaching session to minimize embarrassment and foster candid communication. The tone of the coaching should be positive and encouraging. Coaching is not discipline, it is a collaborative effort to improve driving.

- **Tap your DRM company for tools to use during your implementation.**
  Ask your DRM provider for tools to help acclimate your drivers (and managers) to their new environment. Items such as a video introducing and explaining the solution, as well as template materials for acknowledging that each driver has been trained on the solution or that a coaching session has taken place, will help ensure a smooth transition and a successful program.

## Chapter 8

# You Are What You Drive

Remember Christine, Stephen King's ultimate evil vehicle of horror? She was a white-over-red, two-toned finned survivor of a time when high-test gasoline sold for a quarter a gallon and speed was king.

Does that 1958 Plymouth Fury come to mind when you see people driving with total recklessness, abandonment and disregard for our driving laws? Whether it be speed, lane changes, merges or yields, I'm convinced that cars are simply an extension of the driver's personality.

Which brings me to the point that maybe we should all avoid certain cars—and their drivers—the next time we see them on the highway. It's likely that "how people view the 'personality' of their cars might be a better indication of how aggressive they'll be behind the wheel than their own personalities," says researcher Jacob Benfield of Colorado State University.

Benfield and his colleagues surveyed 204 car-owning college students to measure the degree to which they gave human characteristics to their rides—call it auto-anthropomorphism. They found that about half of all students thought of their car as being masculine or feminine, and more than one in four had named their cars—results consistent with earlier studies of car owners.

The psychologists also gave students standard personality tests and measured their propensity for road rage or aggressive driving. Then they went a step further and asked the students to repeat the personality tests and "imagine that your vehicle had a personality. Now rate the following items based on the vehicle's personality."

They found that drivers who thought of their cars as being male or female "scored significantly higher than non-gender-vehicle drivers on verbal aggression, physical aggression, use of vehicle, driving anger and pejorative labeling/verbally aggressive thinking," Benfield and his colleagues reported in *Personality and Individual Differences.*

When the researchers examined the results of the personality tests, they found that the personality of the car and driver were far from a perfect match. Moreover, they found that the perceived personality of the car sometimes was a better predictor of aggressive driving tendencies than the owner's personality.

For example, people who thought of their car as friendly were more likely to behave better on the road, even if they were not particularly friendly people. "If people perceive their Corolla to be a jerk, they might drive more aggressively than if they thought their Mustang had a nice personality," Benfield said.[1]

In another study, Dr. Charles Kenny, president of The Right Brain People, discovered that you can learn a lot about people simply by noticing the car they drive:

- Mini-van: Need for nurturance and escape
- Two-door sedan for single women: Gender identity
- SUV: Need for adventure
- Hummer and large SUVs: Need for power and control; the "warrior mentality"
- Lexus: Need for status and rejuvenation
- Luxury cars such as Mercedes, BMW, Acura, Infiniti and Cadillac: Need for status, telling themselves that they have arrived as well as telling others!
    For example:
    - Mercedes: Needs for status and power; need for perfection (precision engineering)
    - BMW: Need for status and impulse control

- Ultra-luxury brands, such as Bentley and Rolls Royce: Need for status and uniqueness (Luxury is never having to say it!)
- Convertibles: Need for freedom and independence; need for escape
- Sports cars: Youthful exuberance, rejuvenation, impulse control. For the Corvette, a need for immortality.
- Four-door sedan: Practicality and nurturance
- Mustang V-8 (not the V-6): Impulse control
- Muscle cars such as the old Camaro and Firebird: Impulse control
- Original Volkswagen Beetle: Need for uniqueness and physical security (reliability and low gas mileage)
- New Volkswagen Beetle: Need for rejuvenation
- Trucks: A combination of power, control and gender identity
- Full-size trucks: More about power and control
- Compact trucks: More about gender identity
- Full-size four-door trucks (men): Power, control and gender identity; nurturance
- Full-size four-door trucks (women): Independence and gender identity
- Hybrids: Character; doing the right thing; fear of judgment
- Compact cars: Need for rationality and character
- Honda Fit: Need for rationality; physical security; need for uniqueness
- PT Cruiser: Need for rejuvenation; need for uniqueness
- Custom vans: Need for uniqueness
- VW Bus: Need for community and acceptance[2]

## The Home Is Where the Heart Is ... or the Car!

Now that we know who is behind the wheel based upon the body type on top of the wheels, let's make driving even more interesting. Research shows that 65 percent of drivers stated they eat while driving, according to a PEMCO Insurance poll on driver distraction. Is one food more distracting than another? You bet.

In 2006, a NHTSA study reported that 80 percent of all the nation's car crashes involved some type of driver distraction, with "eating on the run" listed as one of the many distractions that plague motorists today. Though NHTSA doesn't track specific information on food-related distraction, it does track general distractions. Distractions in cars were considered the cause in 25 percent of more than 6.3 million auto crashes, with most collisions occurring within three seconds of a driver being distracted.

The top ten food offenders in a car are:

1. Coffee—It always finds a way out of the cup.
2. Hot soup—Many people drink it like coffee and run the same risks.
3. Tacos—A food that can disassemble itself without much help, leaving your car looking like a salad bar.
4. Chili—The potential for drips and slops down the front of clothing is significant.
5. Hamburgers—From the grease of the burger to ketchup and mustard, it could all end up on your hands, your clothes, and the steering wheel.
6. Barbecued food—The same issue arises for barbecued foods as for hamburgers. The sauce may be great, but if you have to lick your fingers, the sauce will end up on whatever you touch.
7. Fried chicken—Another food that leaves you with greasy hands, which means constantly wiping them on something, even if it's your shirt. It also makes the steering wheel greasy.
8. Jelly or cream-filled donuts—Has anyone eaten a jelly donut without some of the center oozing out?
9. Soft drinks—Not only are they subject to spills, but also the carbonated kind can fizz as you're drinking if you make sudden movements, and most of us remember cola fizz in the nose from childhood. It isn't any more pleasant now.
10. Chocolate—Like greasy foods, chocolate coats the fingers as it melts against the warmth of your skin, and leaves its mark anywhere you touch. As you try to clean it off the steering wheel you're likely to end up swerving.[3]

You can bet that I'll be even more careful the next time I see a guy eating a jelly donut while driving a Corvette. Particularly if he's also drinking coffee!

## What Gives You the Right?

As time becomes more precious and multi-tasking becomes the norm, patience starts to wear thin. You know the type of drivers I'm talking about. They are the ones who cut you off, merge without yielding and those who simply ignore the common courtesies (and laws) that make our roads safer—laws like using turn signals, leaving space between vehicles and slowing down, rather than speeding up.

Aggressiveness is becoming more prevalent in our lives and on our roads. Whoever thought that you'd potentially take your life in your hands by simply leaving your driveway? How important is it that the person behind you (who is now in front of you) gets to their destination one minute—or thirty seconds—earlier than you? Or, is that the real reason they drive so aggressively? Perhaps they just had an argument at home, lost their job, or were defeated in a local soccer match. No matter the reason, they are taking your life into their hands. And you need to be careful. That's why driving defensively is so important.

The National Highway Traffic Safety Administration (NHTSA) defines aggressive driving as, "when individuals commit a combination of moving traffic offenses so as to endanger other persons or property." Some other communities define aggressive driving as "the operation of a motor vehicle involving three or more moving violations as part of a single continuous sequence of driving acts, which is likely to endanger any person or property." By NHTSA's estimates, 56 percent of all highway deaths involve aggressive driving.

Some behaviors typically associated with aggressive driving include: exceeding the posted speed limit, following too closely, erratic or unsafe lane changes, improperly signaling lane changes, failure to obey traffic control devices (stop signs, yield signs, traffic signals, railroad grade cross signals, etc.). Law enforcement agencies should include running red lights as part of their definition of aggressive driving. NHTSA calls the act of running red lights as one of the most dangerous forms of aggressive driving.[4]

One of the major problems with aggressive driving is that it can lead to road rage. Road rage differs from aggressive driving. It is a criminal offense and is "an assault with a motor vehicle or other dangerous weapon by the operator or passenger(s) of one motor vehicle on the operator or passenger(s) of another motor vehicle or is caused by an incident that occurred on a roadway."[5]

Some people say that a vehicle gives the driver a sense of anonymity and power. Perhaps this is the reason people behave the way they do when they get behind the wheel. Maybe their vehicle gives them the opportunity to act out those aggressions they cannot act upon in their day-to-day life. That's why it's even more important to pay attention to the type of vehicles around you—and what the person behind the wheel is doing—since it may tell you more about how that person will behave when they're sharing the road with you.

As for me, I may consider relocating to Minneapolis, Nashville, St. Louis, Seattle or Atlanta. They were recently listed as the cities with the most courteous drivers and the least road rage.[6]

## Learn to Drive Defensively

Driving defensively means not only taking responsibility for yourself and your actions, but also keeping an eye on "the other guy." The National Safety Council suggests the following guidelines to help reduce your risks on the road:

- Don't start the engine without securing each passenger in the car, including children and pets. Safety belts save thousands of lives each year! Lock all doors.
- Remember that driving too fast or too slow can increase the likelihood of collisions.
- Don't kid yourself. If you plan to drink, designate a driver who won't drink. Alcohol is a factor in almost half of all fatal motor vehicle crashes.
- Be alert! If you notice that a car is straddling the center line, weaving, making wide turns, stopping abruptly or responding slowly to traffic signals, the driver may be impaired.
- Avoid an impaired driver by turning right at the nearest corner or exiting at the nearest exit. If it appears that an oncoming car is crossing into your lane, pull over to the roadside, sound the horn and flash your lights.
- Notify the police immediately after seeing a motorist who is driving suspiciously.
- Follow the rules of the road. Don't contest the "right of way" or try to race another car during a merge. Be respectful of other motorists.
- Don't follow too closely. Always use a "four-second following distance."
- While driving, be cautious, aware and responsible.[7]

---

[1] Ricard Morin, *The Washington Post,* 2006

[2] WBZ-TV, February 11, 2007

[3] Hagerty Classic Insurance, Insure.com

[4] nhtsa.gov

[5] Wikipedia

[6] In The Driver's Seat 2006 AutoVantage Road Rage Survey

[7] National Safety Council

## Chapter 9

# Eyes Back on the Road, Young Man!

Have you ever driven along a busy freeway and noticed that the traffic flow had slowed to a crawl and was impeded by something that affected all lanes traveling in a particular direction?

You slowly approach the eventual bottleneck expecting to see road construction or a collision, only to eventually spot a police car driving along thoughtlessly and inconsiderately at the posted speed limit!

How rude. Don't they know we've got places to go, people to see and things to do … all while talking on our cell phones, eating burgers and driving our potentially lethal weapons, too? For those excruciatingly painful few moments while we are in sight of the patrol car, what are we to do? Continue these activities in the slow motion reality of the posted speed limit, too? Some people have no sense of urgency!

Then, thankfully, the police car finally exits the freeway in search of another artery to clog, which allows us to immediately go back to speeding, tailgating, weaving, eating, texting, middle fingering and otherwise, driving "normally."

This annoyingly frequent phenomenon is an example of human behavioral science called the "Hawthorne Effect." The Hawthorne Effect is a well-known, and oft-repeated, story of experiments conducted at an assembly line at the Hawthorne Works, a large factory complex built by Western Electric in Cicero, Illinois. This factory was in existence from 1908 to 1983 and had over 45,000 employees at its height. The experiments that proved the Hawthorne Effect took place between 1924 and 1932.

## It's Not Just the Lighting

When the studies began, the lighting in and around the production line was sparse and dingy, impinging on the workers' ability to see their work. The idea was to brighten the work area in order to increase production. After introducing more lighting, the researchers were pleased to find that, indeed, their theory had worked and production increased nicely with the added light.

Well, if some light was good, then more light would be better. Right? Again, they were rewarded with an even greater output as they increased the lumens.

So now our curious experimenters decided to test for the Law of Diminishing Returns. They increased the lighting level again; this time the light was hot and obnoxiously bright. Surely the assembly line productivity would not continue to increase yet again?

Against all logic, and to their amazement, they found that, indeed, productivity had increased in spite of the extreme lighting conditions, rather than because of them. Thinking this ever-more curious, they decided that maybe the lighting level and the production output were not cause and effect after all. They boldly experimented one more time by removing all of the incremental light they had added and went back to the original low light and dingy conditions that were in place before they started the experiments.

Of course, you can guess what happened next. Production went up again.

The lesson learned, and what has become institutionalized as the Hawthorne Effect, is that it was not the working conditions that drove increased performance. Rather, it was the fact that someone was watching, someone was measuring and someone cared. This is what made the difference.

The other side of this equation is that if you don't watch, don't measure and don't have meaningful consequences, the subtle message you are communicating is that whatever the endeavor, it doesn't really matter. But the message goes far beyond that. If no one is watching, measuring, or if there aren't any consequences, then no one really cares, and anything will do, any outcome is alright, and good enough is good enough. The end result? Why bust your ass for things that don't really matter and that nobody really cares about?

You can say something matters. You can clearly train people as to what you expect from them when they are assembling things or when they are driving. But, if you don't observe what they are doing, measure what they are doing, and don't have consequences for what they are doing, then they don't respond to what you say. The resulting action is that they inject their own interpretation into your actions (or inactions), and deduce that despite what you say, train or threaten, you don't really mean it. Their behavior will revert back to the path of least resistance. In many instances, in fact, their behavior will return to that where they can glean the most reward out of the activity intrinsically for them, absent any formal and certain consequences from you.

## Do the Risks Outweigh the Rewards?
Let's return to our highway example.

Each of us knows with certainty that we are supposed to obey the rules of the road. We are not supposed to speed, drink, eat, drive, weave, bob, or otherwise take undue risks with our life and others' lives when we are behind the wheel. Yet all of us do so with regularity, absent a patrol car within sight.

Oh, we all have our reasons. Circumstances cause us to weigh the risk versus the reward when we are driving and then we behave accordingly. I'm running late, I have to get to work on time and I'm hungry because I missed breakfast. Unlike all those other Bozo drivers out there, I can handle it.

**Fact:** The average driver needs to leave a four-second following distance between himself and the car blocking the path in front of him.

**Fiction:** I know I can handle a one-second gap because, after all, wasn't I the best athlete in the history of my high school thirty years ago? And, have I ever been in an auto accident because I didn't leave a four-second gap? Besides, who will know how I drive except me? These other people just don't know what it's like to be me and don't realize all of the demands on my time. If they were in my shoes and could handle it as well as I can … well, they'd do it, too!

Each year, the fog thickens and our motorist's recollections grow hazy. Each year, the gap grows ever larger between his athletic prowess and the second best guy, and he's only getting better and more invincible as time passes and his memory recreates the past!

So our memory-enhanced motorist reliving his high school glory days is weighing his risk-reward possibilities:

- He's late.
- He needs to make up time.
- His reactions are excellent.
- He can handle it.
- And, the rules are for the other guy.

Besides …

- He won't get caught.
- He'll be alert for police.
- He has a radar detector.
- And everything will turn out all right. It always does.

From a behavioral science point of view, our motorist is calculating that the behavior of speeding and following too closely brings future and uncertain consequences. In this case, it is worth the risk or the bet that he won't get caught or be involved in a crash. It's luck rearing its ugly head once more. He is riding that game of chance, hoping beyond hope, that this won't be the time he gets caught.

### Fixing the Problem

So how do we extinguish this risky behavior? Through coaching and consequences. Whether the driver is a person simply driving to work or the grocery store, a teenager heading to school or a party, or a long- or short-haul truck driver delivering products we need, the process is the same. Coaching and consequences.

Let's first focus on coaching. Coaching needs to be part of an overall process. Improving driver safety and risky driver behavior is an ongoing, continual process. One way to help ensure a successful program is to use the acronym "COACH" to help you build your own program:

C — C-level or other high-level ongoing support from within your organization (or at home).
   • Gain high-level support for the program before launch.
   • Once the program is launched, maintain the support of your high-level advocate(s) by providing ongoing status reports.

O — Open communication with employees (or family members) before and after the program is launched.

**C.O.A.C.H.**

**C** C-level support

**O** Open communication with employees

**A** Application of the process is consistent

**C** Clear set of consequences (negative and positive)

**H** Have someone monitoring the DRM program and measuring the success

   • The program must be properly explained prior to launch. Share all clearly defined expectations with everyone involved.
   • Constant sharing of the program via coaching, training, newsletters and other forms of communication.
   • Post a summary report listing each person's performance. To avoid embarrassment, substitute anonymous ID numbers for each person's name.

A — Application of the process is consistent.
   • Tasks and expectations should be clearly defined.
   • Be vigilant and constant in applying the process. Poor driving behavior tends to return when the program application is sporadic.
   • Be sure the program is properly staffed, including a backup in case of vacation, illness or job change.

C — Clear set of consequences (negative and positive).
- Isolate those excelling or struggling in the program.
- Violations of driving expectations must be addressed with consequences, such as:
    - Coaching, e-mail, voicemail
    - Forms of consequences include:
        - Change to non-driving status
        - Less desirable work assignment
        - Less desirable vehicle
        - Assign for retraining
        - Impact on safety bonus
- Violations of company policy should be followed through per your organization's already existing plan. In most cases, a DRM is just an additional tool to monitor compliance, so no new policies are needed.
- High achievers in the program are acknowledged and rewarded.
    - Use recognition programs or reward programs to acknowledge those with the fewest events or risk points in a specific period.
    - Create a "Good Driving" certification. Use this certificate as a positive recognition tool when exceptional driving behavior is identified.

H — Have a system in place to monitor and evaluate the performance of the person or people administering the program.
- The tasks and expectations for those applying the program should be well-defined.
- The program managers should have a stake in the success or failure of the program. Possible ways to do this include having a compensation package tied to a reduction in cost of collisions or frequency or number of events. Non-monetary ways of accomplishing this include tying the program performance expectations to job performance expectations and including this in periodic performance review.
- Report tracking event reduction (or increase), coaching completion and others should be viewed and discussed on a scheduled basis.

In addition to coaching, your driver needs to have immediate and certain consequences every time he or she exhibits a risky behavior. You need the ability to capture or observe the actual behavior and then tie positive consequences to safe and desired behavior, along with negative consequences to unsafe or risky behavior.

Positive consequences can take many forms, such as dynamic pay or bonuses. In some instances, a simple acknowledgment that a driver did the right thing, someone noticed and they cared is enough. In other words, like the Hawthorne Effect, someone was watching, someone was measuring, someone cared and it mattered. These consequences should occur as close to the actual behavior as possible. Imagine if you ate a piece of chocolate cake and your taste buds and endorphins did not register the good taste and good feelings until late the next week … a weight loss program for sure!

Like the positive consequences, the negative consequences must be administered in the same way. They must be as immediate as possible and certain. Every time the driver chooses to disobey the law or behave in an unsafe manner, he must know that it will be observed, it will be measured, and there will be an unpleasant consequence. Here again, dynamic pay can accomplish this by virtue of paying him at a lower rate than he could make if he were driving responsibly. Or, it can be as simple as a gentle reminder or coaching from a supervisor, peer or anyone who cares.

Ultimately, you need a way to monitor his driving without riding beside him each and every day. This is where an exception-based video event recorder will help you improve your driver's driving skills, reduce his risk of driving irresponsibly, lower your number of incidents and claims, while also increasing your bottom line.

## How Does it Work?

Any significant movement (such as a hard brake, sudden swerve, hard impact) activates the recorder. Since the recorder is always recording, it immediately saves the critical seconds before and after the incident and sends the audio-video recording via cell to a data center for analysis and later viewing over the web. So, whether the driver is talking on a cell phone or suddenly awakes from drowsy driving, the recorder senses the sudden erratic movement or swerving of the vehicle, either forward, back or side to side.

The recorder continuously writes over itself if nothing significant or risky happens. The reward, or the consequence to the driver, is as simple as the recorder will not record anything he does during the day so long as he does it safely. If he follows too closely and has to jam on the brakes, the recorder does not write over the seconds preceding and succeeding the questionable event; they're saved for review and, consequently, he has a slice of his life open to scrutiny. This simple little consequence, alone, makes most of us stay alert and in the moment while driving, thus resulting in safer driving, fewer accidents and dramatic reductions in property loss and casualty.

The nice part about the Hawthorne Effect is that it is just an application of pure behavioral science. It goes to the essence of the human nature that is in every one of us. Once we become adults and move out from under our parents' span of protection, we are defined by the choices we make. We must have meaningful consequences for the choices we make to help us form the guard rails of life that will take us down the various paths that are available to us.

As we set about making our mark on the world, we try to understand the significance of life and the reason we are here so we can make the most of our time on Earth. We want the things we choose to do to be significant and impactful, or at least meaningful, to someone and for some reason.

I can still hear my father's voice saying, "If it's worth doing, it's worth doing well." If I do it and nobody ever noticed, and nobody ever cared, was it still worth doing at all, let alone well? Or, as some would ask, "Does a tree falling in a forest with nobody around to hear it, make a sound?"

I don't know, but that siren and those damn lights in my rear view mirror are sure distracting me from figuring this out!

## What Is Driver Risk Management?

- Driver Risk Management is a behavior-based risk mitigation solution that predicts and prevents actual risky driving behaviors likely to result in collisions.
- Driver behavior directly impacts a fleet's risk factors, safety record and operating costs.
- Companies have little visibility into their drivers' behavior on the road.
- Driver Risk Management dramatically improves a fleet's bottom line by mitigating risk and reducing the costs associated with unsafe driving behaviors.

### Protect Your Drivers

A driver risk management program shows a commitment to driver safety by protecting your drivers from:
- False claims
- Service problems and delays
- Unnecessary turnover

### "Incentivize" Your Drivers

A driver risk management program gives you the opportunity to reward drivers for:
- Fewer crashes
- Less damage
- More on-time deliveries
- Good driving

### Identify and Correct Your Drivers' Habits

A driver risk management program provides drivers with:
- Regular coaching and training to help them learn to drive better
- Better communication between the driver and management
- Positive encouragement and potential incentive

## Chapter 10

# Man versus Machine

Auto manufacturers continue to improve the safety of the vehicles they produce—whether it's by adding seat belts, roll bars and air bags, or advanced technologies such as antilock brakes, stability controls and lane departure warnings. Soon, it might not be uncommon to see vehicles "driving themselves" while passengers chat, listen to satellite radio or fiddle with their BlackBerry. Until that happens, however, automakers inadvertently are putting us at risk.

Don't get me wrong. I'm not opposed to these safety enhancements, nor am I trying to pick a fight with the auto manufacturers. Their intentions are good and the value of their safety innovations is clear. No one will argue, for instance, the significance of seat belts and air bags in reducing traffic fatalities. According to traffic safety researchers and the National Highway Traffic Safety Administration (NHTSA), seat belts reduce a person's chances of dying in a crash by 45 percent and being injured by 50 percent. Seat belts also prevent total ejections from a car during a crash, an important factor in preventing fatalities, since 75 percent of car occupants who are totally ejected during a crash are killed, according to NHTSA. Several independent studies have shown that seat belts also reduce the severity of injury: The odds of serious injury for people not wearing seat belts are four to five times greater than for people who are belted.

In short, research has repeatedly demonstrated what is now widely known: Seat belts save lives and prevent injury. Unfortunately, for a nation arguably more dependent than any other on the car, the U.S. has an occupant safety record that leaves significant room for improvement. Despite recent achievements, the U.S. fares worse in seat belt use and traffic fatality rates when compared to other industrialized nations, including Great Britain, Germany, Sweden, Australia and Canada. Seat belt usage exceeds 90 percent in several of these countries, while the U.S. seat belt use rate is currently 81 percent, an all-time high.[1, 2]

In related good news, the Insurance Institute for Highway Safety recently reported that side air bags that protect people's heads are reducing driver deaths in cars struck on the near (driver) side by an estimated 37 percent.[3]

Recent technologies and innovations in safety devices hold similar promise. In 2006, U.S. lawmakers called for automakers to install electronic stability control (ESC) systems on all passenger cars and trucks by 2012 in an effort to save at least 10,000 lives a year, not to mention the prevention of 168,000 to 252,000 injuries. Auto safety experts describe the stability control system as the single most important vehicle safety improvement since the seat belt. ESC reduces the risk of all single-vehicle crashes by more than 40 percent and fatal crashes by 56 percent, according to the Insurance Institute for Highway Safety.[4] ESC systems use automatic computer-controlled braking of individual wheels to help the driver maintain control in situations where a vehicle without ESC would skid out of control and likely leave the road; nearly all rollover crashes occur after a vehicle leaves the road.

Unfortunately, the safer our vehicles become, the riskier our behavior becomes. We continue to think we're invincible, and allow ourselves to become overconfident and increase our level of risk. "I have an electronic stability control system in my car, so I can take that turn at 70 mph and I'll be fine. I won't lose control or roll my car." Yeah, right.

## A False Sense of Security

If this sounds familiar, it's because it is. It's that same false sense of security mentioned in Chapter Two. As you may remember, consumers adapt to innovations that improve safety by becoming less vigilant about safety. In other words, the article suggests that safety-conscious drivers are more likely than other drivers to purchase vehicles with air bags and antilock brakes, but these safety devices and technologies, alone, do not have a significant impact on collisions or injuries. The suggestion is that drivers trade off enhanced safety for speedier trips. The seatbelt doesn't help prevent crashes at all. It just helps you survive one.

We think we're safer in our technologically advanced automobiles outfitted with air bags, stability controls and all the rest, so we take more chances, drive faster and more aggressively. We paid extra for all these safety features, damn it! Yet, all the vehicle safety features in the world can't protect us from the primary factor in 95 percent of all collisions—ourselves.

The unintended consequence of all of this very good and very effective technology being brought to bear on the crashes and fatalities on our roads, is that people make choices about their behavior based upon expected results. If I can control my car with ever-increasing levels of confidence (and because the car itself responds beautifully to edgy and difficult maneuvers), then I can continue to reinforce the notion that I can push the envelope of risky driving. Why? Because I, and my trusted steed, Silver, can handle it. Every time Silver and I do something edgy and don't roll over or bang into someone or something else, our behavior is reinforced. Until, that is, our luck runs out and it's no longer OK.

Silver, however, is not the problem. It's me. I'm the one in control. My eyes and ears are telling my brain to control which maneuvers at what times based upon my judgment. I am the source of all the mistakes I make on the road. And, you are the source of all the mistakes you make on the road. It's not the vehicle. It's not the road. It's you and me.

Remember: These are not accidents. Accidents are an undesirable or unfortunate happening that occurs unintentionally and usually results in harm, injury, damage or loss. They are mistakes (an error in action, calculation, opinion, or judgment caused by poor reasoning, carelessness, insufficient knowledge) that you and I, as the drivers, make due to a number of root cause errors in judgment.

Therefore, any effective road safety program must start with the driver.

## So Where Do We Begin?

Isn't it ironic that the new father who invested in a luxury station wagon or SUV with the most advanced safety bells and whistles to protect his infant child has a tendency to drive faster or more aggressively because he has greater confidence in his vehicle? Inadvertently, he has become a riskier driver. Just take a look at all of the features in the Volvo Safety Concept Car:

- See-through A-pillars
- "Invisible" B-pillars
- Active rearview mirrors
- Rearward-facing cameras
- Adaptive headlights
- Night vision
- Collision warning sensors
- Lane centering
- Flashing brake lights
- Four-point safety belts

The above features would be enough safety advancements in one concept vehicle to satisfy most manufacturers. But not Volvo. The SCC also includes a number of personal security functions that ensure driver safety beyond the actual driving experience. These are made available to the operator by way of an advanced remote control called the Volvo Personal Communicator (VPC).

The VPC remote unit has a built-in fingerprint sensor that identifies the operator. Not only does this lock out potential unauthorized users of the vehicle, but the remote can be programmed to identify multiple drivers, so an entire family, for instance, can use the same remote, while no one else would be able to access the vehicle. This opens up a whole world of programming functions via the remote. For example, as soon as the remote identifies a driver, the VPC immediately communicates this to the vehicle, whereupon the car automatically adjusts the steering wheel, seating position and more to the settings of that particular driver. By the time the driver slides behind the wheel, the car is ready to go.

Additionally, the remote can be programmed to perform a number of automatic functions, such as emergency notification in the event of an accident.[5]

## Accountability Starts with Number One

Now, imagine a child who has learned to ride a bike with training wheels. More likely than not, she is brave and bold, confident in the two small wheels parallel to her rear tire that stabilize the bicycle and keep her upright. Imagine now how her confidence wanes and she becomes increasingly cautious when the training wheels are removed—conscious that she, alone, is responsible for maintaining her balance.

It is the same way for automobile and fleet drivers. As we drive that old clunker with lap belts and seat backs that don't lock properly, we become much more aware of our vulnerability as vehicles speed by us on the freeway. We miss the air bag warning label on our visor and the familiar angle of the safety belt that crosses our chest and keeps us snuggly in the seat. We feel a little less sure of ourselves and proceed with caution, worried about what would happen if we were involved in a crash.

Safety devices can only help so much. And, they can potentially improve our chances of surviving a collision. But at the end of the day, we're the only ones accountable for our safety—not a seat belt, a black box or an antilock braking device.

- *We* need to maintain stability by driving at a speed appropriate for conditions.
- *We* need to avoid the distractions of cell phones, food and cosmetics.
- *We* need to maintain the appropriate following distance in the correct lane.
- *We* need to know when we're too drowsy, drunk or even angry to drive.

DRM technologies that hold us accountable are the most effective solutions at improving driving safety because they identify and help us eliminate the risky things we do behind the wheel.

Buckle up and allow yourself to feel safer in your vehicle outfitted with stability control sensors. But remember one thing: More than any single safety device or technology, the most effective solution to prevent traffic collisions and deaths is improving driver behavior.

# The Emergence of Telematics

Telematics is the blending of computers and wireless telecommunications technologies, ostensibly with the goal of efficiently conveying information over vast networks to improve a host of business functions or government-related public services. The term has evolved to refer to automobile systems that combine global positioning satellite (GPS) tracking and other wireless communications for automatic roadside assistance and remote diagnostics.

Major automakers are equipping new prototype vehicles with wireless-based services controlled by voice commands. This kind of telematics could enable motorists to perform a variety of wireless functions, such as accessing the Internet, receiving or sending e-mail, downloading digital audio and video files or obtaining "smart" transportation information.

The telematics industry is not limited to automotive applications. Other applications are being studied or developed for monitoring water and air pollution, for medical informatics and health care, and for distance learning. Many European countries are developing uniform policies to integrate telematics applications into government, business and education.

While there are many potential applications for vehicle telematics, the main advantage for transportation safety advocates is that it will help reduce, and ideally eliminate, road injuries and road traffic related deaths worldwide. When used in a commercial environment, vehicle telematics can potentially be a powerful and valuable tool to improve the efficiency of an organization. Some practical applications of vehicle telematics include:

- Vehicle tracking
- Trailer tracking
- Satellite navigation
- Mobile data and mobile television
- Wireless vehicle safety communications
- Emergency warning system for vehicles
- Intelligent vehicle technologies
- Car clubs
- Auto insurance

# Top Ten Safety Technologies

It's just a fact of life—we are living longer. And it's not just because of tofu, sunscreen and medical breakthroughs. Automakers are to thank (or curse) for this as much as doctors, since they are competitively blending performance and creature comforts with cutting-edge safety technology that tries to stay one step ahead of you—and everyone else on the road.

While pedestrian-friendly bumpers and cars that can drive themselves may seem like the faraway future of automotive safety, so did many of the features that are now industry standards for this year's models. It makes us wonder if the Jeep Grand Cherokee Concierge concept from 2002—with an integrated heart defibrillator—might catch on as part of the next wave of safety.

Below are Edmund's top ten choices for safety technologies:

1.  **Tire-pressure monitoring**

    The National Highway Traffic Safety Administration has required that all U.S. passenger vehicles weighing 10,000 pounds or less be equipped with a tire-pressure monitoring system by the 2008 model year. Sensors at the wheels are able to alert you if the air pressure is too low by an audible warning, a light on the instrument panel, or both.

2.  **Adaptive cruise control/collision mitigation**

    Modern cruise control goes beyond just maintaining a constant speed. Thanks to sensors and the use of radar, cruise control can now adjust the throttle and brakes to keep a safe distance from the vehicle in front of you if there are changes in traffic speed or if a slowpoke cuts in. If the system senses a potential collision, it typically will brake hard and tighten the seat belts. Once it knows the lane is clear or traffic has sped up, it will return your car to its original cruising speed, all without your input.

3.  **Blind-spot detection/side assist/collision warning**

    This technology is designed to alert you to cars or objects in your blind spot during driving or parking, or both. Usually it will respond when you put on your turn signal; if it detects something in the way, it may flash a light in your mirror, cause the seat or steering wheel to vibrate, or sound an alarm.

### 4.  Lane-departure warning/wake-you-up safety

This is similar to blind-spot/side-assist technology, but with more range. It judges an approaching vehicle's speed and distance to warn you of potential danger if you change lanes. It can also warn if it determines your car is wandering out of the lane, which could be useful if you become distracted. This could come in the form of a vibration through the seat or steering wheel, or an alarm. Down the road, expect lane-departure warning to even be able to monitor body posture, head position and eye activity to decide if the driver is falling asleep and the vehicle is behaving erratically.

### 5.  Rollover prevention/mitigation

Most automakers offer an electronic stability control system, and some offer a *preparation* system (seat belts tighten, rollbars extend). However, what we're talking about is more intelligent than that. If the system senses a potential rollover (such as if you whip around a corner too fast or swerve sharply), it will apply the brakes and modulate throttle as needed to help you maintain control.

### 6.  Occupant-sensitive/dual-stage air bags

All humans are not created equal, and air bags are evolving to compensate in the form of low-risk, multistage and occupant-sensitive deployment. Technology can now sense the different sizes and weights of occupants as well as seat belt usage, abnormal seating position (such as reaching for the radio or bending to pick something off the floor), rear-facing child seats and even vehicle speed.

### 7.  Emergency brake assist/collision mitigation

This brake technology is different from an antilock braking system or electronic brakeforce distribution, in that it recognizes when the driver makes a panic stop (a quick shift from gas to brake pedal) and will apply additional brake pressure to help shorten the stopping distance. It may also work in conjunction with the smart cruise control or stability control system in some vehicles if it senses a potential collision.

### 8.  Adaptive headlights and/or night-vision assist

Night vision can be executed in different forms, such as infrared headlamps or thermal-imaging cameras. But no matter the science, the goal is the same: to help you see farther down the road and to spot animals, people or trees in the path—even at nearly 1,000 feet away. An image is generated through a cockpit display, brightening the objects that are hard to see with the naked eye. Adaptive headlights follow the direction of the vehicle (bending the light as you go around corners). They may also be speed-sensitive (changing beam length or height), or compensate for ambient light.

## 9. Rearview camera

Rearview cameras not only protect your car, but also protect children and animals from accidental back-overs. Backing up your car has graduated from side mirrors tilting down or causing chirps and beeps to real-time viewing. New-school tech involves a camera that works with the navigation system to provide a wide-open shot of what's happening behind you to help with parking or hooking up a trailer.

## 10. Emergency response

There are a variety of ways vehicles now, and in the future, will handle an emergency situation. For example, DaimlerChrysler's Enhanced Accident Response Systems (EARS) turns on interior lighting, unlocks doors and shuts off fuel when air bags deploy, while Volkswagen's also switches on the hazards and disconnects the battery terminal from the alternator. In addition, GM's OnStar and BMW Assist both alert their respective response centers of the incident and make crash details available to emergency personnel.

---

[1] Prevention Institute 2002

[2] NHTSA Traffic Safety Facts, November 2006

[3] McCartt AT; Kyrychenko SY. 2007. Efficacy of side airbags in reducing driver deaths in driver-side car and SUV collisions. Traffic Injury Prevention 8: 162–170.

[4] Farmer CM. 2006. Effects of electronic stability control: an update. Traffic Injury Prevention 7: 319–324.

[5] Edmunds.com

Chapter 11

# All in an Instant—Those Critical Last (Three) Seconds

Sometimes my two youngest children, Andrew and Caroline, will ask me:

> "Daddy, what is it like after you die?"
> "Is there a heaven?"
> "Are you and Mommy going to die?"
> "How old will I be when I die?"

Since the beginning of thought, mankind has tried in vain to answer these age-old questions of existence and purpose while struggling with the concept of nothingness or contemplating what, if anything, it is like after we die.

Death is a very dark, morose, uncomfortable subject that most of us avoid like … well, like death.

It is much more positive, hopeful, inspiring and useful to focus on life—how we choose to spend it, what we can accomplish and how we will contribute and impact the world around us.

And in fact, that's what those of us lucky enough to work in the DRM industry get to do. We focus on life and the living. We take pride in knowing that our efforts can contribute to making our roads and the driving experience just a little bit safer for everyone. We get excited when an obvious menace is taken off the roads. We feel great when a teenager, who starts out with a very high risk profile, turns into a sane, seasoned and responsible young adult. We become especially gratified when we exonerate a hard-working professional driver who busts his or her butt every day making sure the people, products and services we all count on get safely to where they need to be when they need to be there.

In short, we deal in truth, hope and inspiration. We are the lucky ones. Because in this day and age, with all of the misinformation, disinformation, cheating, lying, spinning and avoiding responsibility we get inundated with, working in the truth industry is a real and rare honor.

One such truth, however, is that sometimes, despite our best efforts, coaching, intervention and awareness, some of those mommies, daddies, and even some of those children, won't make it home.

## The Ugly ... But True Facts

As you may remember, on our roads here in the United States, almost 43,000 of us don't make it home every year. Unfortunately, the European Region experiences close to 127,000 deaths annually on their roads.

These numbers are overwhelming. And to most of us, they're simply statistics. We don't even think about them unless we're individually impacted through family, friends or colleagues. Unfortunately, or fortunately, my colleagues and I see the consequence of these horrors each and every day. Through the process of providing a Driver Risk Management Program, we see more than 500,000 video clips per month. That's half a million examples of risky driving or near misses every single month!

But it's also 500,000 opportunities to coach. That means 500,000 chances to improve. And 500,000 root cause behaviors that can be extinguished and eliminated forever so that all of our odds to get home to those we love, improve substantially.

You may have seen some of the more famous examples on television or on the Internet, but we see things that most people will never see or even imagine:

- We see people falling asleep while operating large vehicles at high speeds.
- We see people robbing drivers at gun point.
- We see drive-by shootings.
- We see people talking on cell phones—as bad as or worse than drinking in many cases.
- We see people following too closely.
- We see road rage.
- We see blank stares.
- We see a failure to look ahead or to leave an out.
- We see mirrors and blind spots not checked.
- We see weaving and speeding. Oh, do we see weaving and speeding!

And we also see seat belts not utilized … often!

Most parents think that seat belt use is a given and a non-negotiable aspect of driving; but the video evidence exposes that as a fallacy. The facts speak for themselves. The major reason teens are killed or seriously injured when involved in traffic crashes is a lack of safety belt use.[1, 2] The Fatality Analysis Reporting System[3] shows that more than two thirds of teen occupants killed in crashes were not wearing safety belts.[4] According to the 2003 Motor Vehicle Occupant Safety Survey sponsored by NHTSA, teen drivers are less likely to wear a safety belt "all the time" (79 percent) than older drivers (84 percent).[5] According to various NHTSA-sponsored state and national safety belt surveys, young people sixteen to twenty-four are observed wearing safety belts at rates 5–15 percent below rates for older people.[6, 7] Numerous surveys conducted in high school parking lots indicate typical teen seat belt use is about 50–60 percent, depending upon the state and the school,[8] but that rate of seat belt use among teens varies dramatically based on age, gender, race and urban/rural setting and region of the country.

Then, there are distractions of every imaginable type: food, drink, navigation, passengers and even text messaging. It's hard to believe that only nine states have considered legislation banning driving while texting (DWT) with only one, Washington, passing a law making DWT a crime with a $101 fine. The reasons we continue these distractions are pretty basic and pretty simple. As humans, we tend to do things differently when people are watching than when we think no one will ever see or know. The old adage is that we …

## Get What We Inspect, Not What We Expect

As if all of these distractions aren't enough, we now add to the mix our culture's expectation that we be available and in communication 24/7. Before we know it, we've now adapted to the new reality that this subtlety imposes upon all of us. We are all multi-taskers.

Having that constant 24/7 pressure to be in touch was previously a skill required only of the very few. But, who among us now has the luxury to take an uninterrupted vacation, enjoy a baseball game or even drive from the office to the airport without several calls and text messages following and dogging us?

Come on, be honest with yourself. Can you actually say you have never done any of the things mentioned above when you were behind the wheel of your vehicle? If you're like the majority of the population, of course you have. Now you may take the occasional chance behind the wheel when you are certain it is safe to do so. You may have even taken extreme risks and, to this day, will swear that it wasn't risky at all. After all, you were there and no one else was, so who could assess that risk better than you?

You might take calculated risks because you had a reason. You looked, it was clear, and you couldn't be late again. So what if you had to cut across those lanes. No problem this time. It was clearly worth it. No one was injured, you weren't late and you're here to tell about it, right?

Wrong.

## Those Three Critical Seconds

Here's the thing we know and you couldn't possibly even imagine …

The last three seconds before a severe crash or a fatality are a crucial and common theme. Those last three seconds are all it takes. People are driving along and almost always multi-tasking with the normal expectation that the tasks they have performed flawlessly thousands of times before will end up the same as always … uneventfully.

We have conditioned ourselves to project the same outcomes from the same inputs we have experienced over thousands of repetitions and even years of safe, uneventful driving.

The scenario is absolutely frightening. You see a driver smiling, laughing and talking one second, and then three seconds later, because he or she reached for a cell phone, turned to address a passenger, took a bite of a hamburger or became involved in any other innocuous distraction from the main task at hand, the windshield spiders into a thousand new patterns. The body goes limp, the breath is gone and that mommy, daddy or daughter is not returning home that night, or any other night.

What I'm trying to convey to you is this: By virtue of having a unique vantage-point that most people will never have or see, I know those little distractions have fatal consequences.

The driver never sees it coming. And never will.

But, with full video and audio playback capability, you see the danger entering the field of view. Inherently, it makes you want to reach out to the driver, to shake them, wake them, stop them and alert them to their impending fate even though you know you are reacting to a *fait accompli*.

Those silly, stupid last three seconds.

## If Only ...
… you hadn't allowed your concentration to drift.
… you hadn't taken that sip of coffee.
… you hadn't looked at that message.
… you hadn't taken that cell call.
… you hadn't texted while driving.

The list goes on and on. It happens so fast that it is absolutely frightening. Sometimes, after I've seen an especially dramatic replay, for just a brief fleeting moment, I swear I'm not going to drive anymore. It happens so fast and with such force and surprise, it must be as instantaneous and unsuspecting as when a butterfly merges with your windshield. The impact of seeing these images replay in my mind is like watching an old movie. A horror movie. One that I'd like to forget, but can't.

Then reality sets in and, of course, not driving or not commuting is not an option.

Where the hope and inspiration comes from, though, is that for every one of those horrible tragedies where you wanted to reach back into time, shake the driver and alert her to her impending demise, there are thousands of those intervention moments where we actually are doing exactly that. We see the patterns and we know that those risky driving behaviors are repeated over and over until someone's luck runs out. Except in these cases, with the help of an audio and video event recording, we can reach in, intervene and make a difference. We can change fate and alter patterns. We can get more mommies and daddies to make it home every night. We can make a difference.

But, it takes prevention and intervention. We are an instant gratification society, and we're not great at disciplining ourselves to behave in healthful, preventative manners. So smoke if you must, eat that double cheeseburger and exercise some other day. But when you are behind the wheel, remember that old refrain, "Hey Buddy, can you spare three seconds?"

Heaven can wait.

# Can Habits Really Be Changed?

The last three seconds are the critical difference between life and death. Here are actual quotes from parents and companies who implemented a Driver Risk Management Program, which used behavior modification to change driving habits and save lives:

### Janet Denn, Parent
"It was not that we distrusted her, but we could use the videos to point out behaviors, such as distractions, that could make her a better driver. Our daughter became a much better driver from the program. She is so much more aware."

### Mark Frahm, Parent and School Board Chair
"As a school board chair, I helped approve one of the first programs … It demonstrated our commitment to student safety and community outreach. Plus, my daughter participated and became a much safer driver."

### Dan Ireland, Parent
"It was a great learning experience for both the kids and the parents. It is a great teaching tool."

### Lynda Kruse, Parent
"Knowing that he was a little bit more conscientious than the other teens, and that he was a good driver out there, was beneficial. When they are out late at night, it's a little easier sitting home. You sleep a little better."

### Dan Brandt, Parent
"You can tell your teen that they took a corner too fast, and they would argue that they didn't. But you can't argue with a video. So from that standpoint alone it was that impartial third party that had no opinion. It gave the true facts."

### Richard D'Orazio, Parent
"I believe this has saved his life and anyone who rides with him. Flat out."

### Emily, Teen Participant
"It worked out to be an advantage for me. Once I learned how to stop triggering the camera, I used the lack of recordings to bargain for more nights out and a later curfew. That part was great."

**Brian, Teen Participant**
"I knew I could do whatever it would take to not trigger the camera, and I wanted that car. It turned out OK. My dad ended up triggering it more times than I did!"

**Paul, Teen Participant**
"I figured out how to beat the system. If I slowed down and paid attention to what other drivers were doing, I hardly ever triggered it."

**Michael Belcher, director of safety at DS Waters,** *which produces and distributes bottled water products throughout the United States*
"One of the first trends we identified is that employees we thought were good drivers because of their accident-free driving records often were the ones speeding, running red lights and behaving most aggressively behind the wheel. It was apparent that while they had not been involved in any accidents to date, they were truly 'accidents waiting to happen' and required coaching to improve their risky driving behaviors. We had no idea the volume of cell phone use was so high. We knew our drivers were using them, but we didn't realize to what extent."

**Drew Jones, vice president of safety and security, Veolia Transportation,** *the largest non-governmental transit provider in the country*
"Safety is a cornerstone of our organization. The solution complements our internal safety programs and takes them to the next level. We can now review near-misses and provide coaching and customized training prior to an incident occurring. We're also able to identify trends, such as repeated hard braking and modify behavior accordingly. I have been in the transportation safety business for a long time and the solution, when managed correctly, is one of the best safety solutions to have been developed in a decade."

**Herb De La Porte, vice president of operations, LifeCare Ambulance**
"Now, you can see the disappointment when the recorder is triggered. Our drivers are professionals and take their driving responsibilities seriously. Overall, they experience greater peace of mind with the recorders because they know they won't be falsely accused in the event of an accident."

**Bill Schoolman, president, Classic Transportation,** *the eighth largest integrated ground transportation provider in the United States*
"Before the program, we could only review accidents. But the program allows us to measure behavior and identify drivers who are at risk for an accident so we can prevent them. I am so happy with the program that I have introduced it to all of our key customers as a way to show them our commitment to safety."

**David Seelinger, president, Empire International,** *the third largest provider of chauffeured transportation in the U.S.*
"The number of accidents is down, and this is not an exaggeration, by 62 percent. Our insurance claims were $650,000 annually before the program. After the first year, they dropped by 50 percent to $325,000. In the second year, there was an additional 50 percent reduction, down to $180,000. I am not trying to promote a product, but it has saved us literally hundreds of thousands of dollars in reduced collisions."

**Jamie Ogle, president, Lloyd Pest Control,** *a premier pest elimination company*
"Some of our drivers were skeptical at first. However, during a recent survey, a majority of our drivers admitted that they had changed driving behaviors, such as driving more slowly over speed bumps. Many have even noticed that their driving habits have improved off the job."

[1-8] "A Conceptual Framework for Reducing Risky Teen Driving Behaviors Among Minority Youth," P. Juarez, D.G. Schlundt, I. Goldzweig, N. Stinson, Jr., *Injury Prevention* 2006

## Chapter 12

# My Bodyguard Better Be Wearing His Seat Belt

I grew up in a north side Chicago neighborhood near Wrigley Field where, of course, the Cubs play. Very near there is the high school I attended named Lakeview because, apparently, at one time long before extensive land reclamation and a lot of tall buildings were built, you could see Lake Michigan from there. Don't even try to see the lake now.

My mother went there, too. I learned to drive there. I also learned a lot of other things there, but that's for another book. I have a lot of fond memories of those long-ago days, even though I have been gone for thirty-five years.

Recently, I was poolside at a resort in Scottsdale, Arizona. A man, his wife and three children came in, several of them donning Cubs' hats. Being the astute observer that I am, I concluded they must also be from my hometown. Of course, a conversation ensued and, at one point, the man asked me if I knew coach so-and-so from Lakeview High School.

Startled at hearing the name of the man who taught the driver's education class I took thirty-some years ago, I quickly came back to the moment and indicated that I did know him. We then reflected on what a truly small world it has become. After the obligatory "wait till next year" exhortations required of all Cub fans, we waved goodbye.

Now, I am not one especially inclined to believe in fate, universal karma or even "things happening for a reason." But, I couldn't help but reflect on what a strange coincidence it was to …

- Run into a man from my hometown in a place 1,800 miles away,
- Who happens to bring up the name of the man who taught me to drive thirty-some years ago,
- While I am currently the CEO of a company that makes its living by coaching others to drive better. Or, at least to do so with the least possible risk.

Of all the gin joints in all the towns in all the world, she walks into mine …

Oh no, wait. Wrong movie.

It did get me thinking, however, about another movie, *My Bodyguard*. It came out about twenty-five years ago. And, to the best of my knowledge, it is the only movie ever to be filmed at my old high school, Lakeview.

Although they didn't call the school Lakeview in the movie, it was definitely filmed there. It was exciting to see the smallish teen-age actor bullied by Matt Dillon while others got pushed around in my old hallways and threatened in my old lunchroom. That teenage actor, whose name I've long forgotten, was plastered against the very same set of lockers as mine and chased down the same streets and alleys as I was. A "yoot" in the 1960s of the first Mayor Daley's City of Broad Shoulders.

## That's Not Me

Another coincidence with *My Bodyguard*? Some of you may think so. I'm not so sure. But, it made me think about what many drivers think about video event recorders and their initial reaction to the concept. Although they may initially find it uncomfortable or obtrusive, they usually conclude that they like it and consider it their own personal bodyguard. In fact, I've been told that they even feel naked or unprotected without it.

It usually begins with:

> "I don't want some camera watchin' what I do when I drive."
> "That's Big Brother."
> "I already know how to drive."
> "I'm a good driver. I don't need it."

I'm always fascinated by the transition that occurs once their vehicle is equipped with a video event recorder. Without fail, the driver's perception immediately starts to change.

- *First*, the camera's G-force trigger is exceeded.
- *Next*, the recorder (which is always filming and recording, but not saving those recordings unless, and until, the G-force sensor tells it to) saves those critical few seconds.
- *Then,* the driver notices the red light on the recorder flashing and indicating that it is going to save this particular slice of their life for observation.

Now it is true that we all know how to drive. We are all licensed. We are all mostly experienced. And many of us have never been in a collision. So, this whole process is just intrusive nonsense!

But, have you ever seen yourself on film or heard your voice recorded? It's a strange sensation, isn't it? Seeing and hearing yourself for the first time as others see and hear you. It is strange and can make you self-conscious. Most of us are overly critical of the view from outside our own perspective, but one thing is for certain. The video recorder is objective and the camera doesn't lie.

## The First Time

It is incredibly consistent when a new driver views his or her events for the first time. Their eyes widen, their mouths drop open slightly and they ask to see the clips over and over again. They can't believe what they're seeing. Then they state that if they weren't seeing it for themselves, with their own eyes, they would swear that the stop sign they ran was never there.

They watch as they follow too closely or fail to anticipate the move another driver two cars ahead was going to make. Or, they keep replaying the few critical seconds where they box themselves in and leave no way to get out of a jam.

They watch it and watch it and watch it in amazement and disbelief. They will slow it down, zoom in and zoom out on a frame. They will see for the very first time, the whole picture. The entire event with both the inside and outside perspective that they couldn't possibly have seen the instant it was happening, let alone recall it correctly.

But that's not all. Not long after this moment of truth is revealed, another magic moment occurs. They start to understand. They start to comprehend. And it all becomes clear. That slow realization of what trips the trigger for the recorder to save the recording. They're beginning to get it. They get the feel of when the G-force has been exceeded and they inherently look up at the recorder. And, without coaxing or coaching, they begin to speak to it as though they were talking to my old driver's education teacher from thirty years ago.

"Sorry about that." "Oops, I didn't mean to do that." Or whatever they would say to the companion, the truth-teller, the teacher, the cop or the supervisor who is always there to protect them, to keep them alert and focused. The one who always tells them the truth, but never speaks.

But you know what else always happens?

They learn to game the system. They begin to realize that the old reliable bodyguard who is always sitting there mute, can be fooled. He can be beaten at this game.

They simply learn how not to trip the trigger.

They leave an out. They anticipate. They slow down more gently. They wear their seat belts and they signal their turns. They watch out for the other guy so they do not have to course correct at the last minute. They simply drive in a manner that does not require what has now become their old friend and mentor to tell them the truth in the first place.

Now don't tell anybody, but that ends up making him or her much safer and less costly as a driver. In fact, my experience with over 1,500 companies in nearly 100,000 vehicles over ten years is that he or she will reduce both the frequency and the severity of their risky driving by at least 50 percent. In fact, most will reduce their frequency and severity of incidents by 60 to 70 percent, while the extreme end of the bell curve comes in at up to 90 percent. They quickly realize that nothing else comes remotely close in helping to correct their driving skills.

One teenager who was enrolled in a DRM program came to this realization and said it best:

*"You can totally cheat how the system works.*

*"1) Since the system has an accelerometer in it, it is vulnerable to gentle movements. It doesn't record anything at all unless you trip the accelerometer.*

*"2) When accelerating from a red light, instead of stomping on the accelerator, which they're totally expecting, step on it gently and gradually until you reach a good cruising speed—the system totally won't know what hit it (it thinks it's standing still).*

*"3) When entering into traffic, you can cheat off the other guy—if you watch what other people are doing ahead of you, you can completely avoid surprises altogether—if you avoid situations where you have to slam on the breaks, you totally won't set off the system and you'll rob it of its precious video.*

*"4) Don't run into stuff. This really should be number one. Bumping into anything (curbs, posts, other cars, cattle, etc.) will set off the system.*

*"OH, and really important to know is that YOUR PARENTS CANNOT SEE YOU ALL THE TIME WITH THE SYSTEM. The only time they EVER get to look at any video of you in your car is when you set it off—then they have a twenty-second look at whatever you're up to in the car.*

*"Some good advice: If you're riding with your stupid friends and they wanna do crap in your car that they wouldn't do in theirs, you have a good reason to tell them not to. I can't tell you how many kids I've seen get busted because they were doing something dumb in someone else's car when the system went off.*

*"The best revenge is simply not to drive like a dick. Then your parents won't have any video to watch, they'll think it's a total waste, and then in like three years, when you're statistically not dead, they'll get rid of the thing. And you're laughin' all the way to the bank."*

## The Evolution of Realization

So, now we have evolved from the initial state of mind that starts with, "I am safe and don't need this" to the realization of "Holy Cow, I wouldn't have believed it if I hadn't seen it with my own eyes" to driving more safely and aware by staying "in the moment."

Once you have transitioned to learning from an objective viewpoint, as to what constitutes being really safe behind the wheel to then never having your bodyguard flash red at you, it becomes a game or a challenge to always "keep it in the green," As our savvy teenager so succinctly stated, if there are no risky driving events to review, the camera never flashes red and always stays in a steady state green light.

Once and for all, you know objectively and for sure that you are behaving in a safe and responsible manner. All this constant companion, your bodyguard, ever really wanted to do in the first place was to keep you safe and keep you alive. The result? You begin to rely on it.

Sound far-fetched?

It's not. Most of our drivers feel unprotected driving a vehicle without the Driver Risk Management program protecting them. If they should get into a tangle, get accused of road rage or damage—or any other false accusation—the camera is there to protect them by always telling the truth. But if you really do know how to drive and you are doing so safely, the only time you will ever see or hear from your bodyguard is when you need the truth to exonerate you. And that's the essence of a bodyguard, isn't it?

## What Goes 'Round, Comes 'Round

I am embarrassed to admit that it took a stranger in a chance encounter to get me to recall the name of the man who taught me to drive all those years ago. If I couldn't remember his name without someone else stating it, what made me think that I remembered the lessons he taught me?

More importantly, I had been driving for over thirty years and was incorporating all of the multi-tasking I thought I had learned to do. Things that weren't even invented when he taught me to drive. Of course, I thought I was a good and safe driver. Just like everyone else.

I could engage in all sorts of risky driving behavior because no one was watching and no one was measuring. I never got caught so I had convinced myself that I could handle risks others couldn't. No one could drive as well as me. And I would never get caught. I was invincible.

My bodyguard was not there to tell me the truth, hold me accountable for my actions or protect me from the irresponsible acts of others. It took a chance encounter with a ghost from the past to show me a glimpse of what might become of the ghost of my future if I didn't become aware of my behavior in the present.

Oops! There I go drifting off into the wrong movie again. Good night, Bob Cratchett.

---

### Recognizing and Rewarding Safe Driving Behavior

Have you ever driven by a construction job site on your daily commute and noticed a sign applauding workers for consecutive accident-free days on the job? The sign might have read something like, "This job site … fifty-six days without an injury accident." Maybe you didn't notice, but someone else did and thought enough of this fact to announce it publicly.

Like those at home, incidents on a job site cost time and money. Far worse, they contribute to the deaths or debilitating injuries of workers. Depending on the severity of an incident, construction companies may face delays in getting work completed, be forced to pay safety-code violation fines and workers' compensation fees, suffer downtime and idle equipment costs and more. Therefore, a commitment to safety from each and every worker on the site is vital to the successful completion of the construction job.

Recognizing workers for incident-free days on the job through a public display, such as that referenced above or more discreet methods, such as bonuses, are important ways to acknowledge workers' commitment to the safety goals of the company and reinforce continued safe behaviors.

Think about your own organization and the vehicles bearing your company name. Yours may be an organization that specializes in cable, utilities or public transport. You want your employees to know how to lay cable properly, repair a damaged line quickly and operate a bus responsibly. But, your employees' driving behavior—just as much as their ability to lay cable, repair a damaged power line or operate a bus—is an equally important competency that directly impacts your corporate reputation, your employees' own safety and the safety of those who share the roadways with them.

You understand the importance of providing employees with the right training—whether to help them perform the routine functions of their job, operate a specialized piece of equipment, or make sales calls. You provide feedback on their performance, identify areas for improvement and reward achievements.

But, what about your employees' driving behavior? Do you provide them with the right driver training? If they operate company vehicles, shouldn't their driving behavior be considered in their performance reviews? Their behavior behind the wheel impacts your organization just as significantly as their behavior on the job site, in front of a customer or during a service call. So, why not review and reward it accordingly?

Tying rewards and recognition to incidents not happening, i.e., daily public recognition for avoiding accidents, in a timely manner is crucial. Doing so helps workers internalize the good behavior. The behavior then shifts from the extrinsic ("I'm operating safely because my employer demands that I do so and recognizes me for demonstrating safe behaviors") to the intrinsic ("I'm operating safely because I care and safety is something I value"). In the latter instance, employees have internalized the behavior and made it part of their own value system.

Recognize and reward your employees for driving safely. Watch what they're doing behind the wheel. If they're demonstrating risky driving behaviors, identify those behaviors, call them on it and help them improve. If they're driving safely and taking measures to avoid an incident, i.e., remaining vigilant, avoiding distractions, not tailgating, etc., recognize them for their diligence. Let them know their behavior matters, it has meaning and you care.

The dynamic pay model is one way to motivate employees. Tie driving performance directly to compensation and allow top-performing employees who demonstrate safe driving behavior to earn at the top of their pay scale. In time, the behavior will become habit and companies will no longer need to motivate employees with praise/money/time off/gifts. Employees will have internalized the behavior and will drive safely because *they* care.

Take a moment to reflect. What are you doing to recognize and reward your employees' safe driving behavior?

## Chapter 13

# Death and Taxes

As the old saying goes, "Nothing can be said to be certain, except death and taxes."

In business, sometimes we get caught up in thinking of certain "fixed" costs as being as unavoidable as death and taxes. Things like rent, taxes and insurance. The danger in this assumptive thinking is, of course, that standards are not challenged and as a result, better, cheaper, safer and faster ways of doing things are not explored—and not even thought about.

So here is an example of an accepted way of life that is crying out to be noticed and challenged. In 1996 (the most recent data available), there were 486 million cars registered worldwide, and 185 million trucks and buses, for a worldwide total of 673 million motor vehicles running around and crashing into one another.

Now get this: It was predicted that if the existing trends (at that time) continued, that number would double in the next thirty years. So, in 2030, we would see 1.2 billion cars, trucks and buses.[1] Not to anyone's surprise, the number *is* growing, as stated by the WorldWatch Institute, which reported that the world's passenger car fleet hit 531 million in

2002. A quarter of these cars were in the United States, a country with just five percent of the world's population. Interestingly, the average car in the U.S. travels 10 percent more each year than a car in the United Kingdom, about 50 percent more than one in Germany and almost 200 percent more than a car in Japan.

With so many vehicles on the road, the underlying assumption, or normative accepted practice here, is that if you drive, accidents will happen. That's why they are called accidents. They are not purposeful. Nobody means to damage your car, put your passenger in the hospital or kill you. They are—pure and simple—"an undesirable or unfortunate happening that occurs unintentionally and usually results in harm, injury, damage or loss."[2]

In today's world, these unfortunate or undesirable happenings occur to the tune of 1.2 million fatalities, 50 million injuries, and $518 billion in property and casualty losses each year.

This is an unfortunate reality of driving in today's world. That's why we have insurance. Like death and taxes, those insured losses are anticipated and costs are calculated up front and collected in advance for the inevitable crash or death you will cause or experience. But why does insurance cost so much?

It boils down to one word: risk.

To an auto insurance company, you are a collection of risks. Your sex, age, marital status, driving record, type of car and place of residence all contribute to an insurer's prediction of whether you'll file a claim.

An insurance company can't know, for certain, what kind of driver you are. They can only guess, based on the accumulated statistics for drivers like you. Even if you're a stellar driver, but happen to be young, single, male and own a sports car, the insurer is probably going to place you in a category with a high premium—or it may reject you entirely.[3]

All because of risk. What is your exposure to the chance of injury or a loss? What's the likelihood you may be involved in a collision … whether it's your fault or someone else's? And how can you make a difference?

## Challenging Conventional Wisdom

So, here's where I want to challenge conventional wisdom. Those injuries, damages and fatalities didn't just happen. That insurance rate you're paying isn't based upon some actuary's whim. There is always a root cause and it is almost never the vehicle behaving independently of the driver. Ninety-nine percent of the time, the root cause of all that carnage and "fixed" cost is the human being who is (or isn't) in control of the car.

Let me challenge another assumption that has evolved into conventional wisdom or common sense. They are not just bad drivers, idiots or stupid people controlling those weapons of mass destruction. They are normal, intelligent, legal and licensed drivers, like you and me, who are simply behaving badly for that particular moment because they can. It's also because, for the 50 million times in a year that a crash did actually happen, there were 500 million times when by pure luck, the same risky driving behavior produced no tangible consequence.

What if, however, driving behavior really was measurable and had consequences before it led to costly tragedies? What if we didn't accept behaviors that were unsafe as normative? And what if we didn't allow one another to behave in ways that put us, our property and loved ones at risk of injury or death?

I've seen thousands of examples where a video event recorder has been used as an observation platform to keep drivers focused on the job at hand, while also reducing property loss and casualty for their employers by 50 percent. I've also seen thousands of examples where a video event recorder has helped save lives by preventing someone from exhibiting the kind of behavior that causes collisions.

As you know by now, the concept is very simple and plays to the laws of human nature. The video event recorder is recording inside and outside the vehicle continuously 24/7, constantly re-recording over the same portion of tape as long as nothing significant or risky happens. The video event recorder just keeps rolling along minding its own business and protecting you from false accusations or liabilities if something were to cause damage or injury, and it really wasn't your fault. Once a significant event occurs, the video event recorder is "triggered" and the critical seconds of event footage are saved for later review. Good or bad, the inside and outside recording will provide the objective unbiased truth, whatever that may be. The truth may or may not set you free, but it will, at minimum, save you the cost of a crash investigation, reconstruction and litigation.

Once an unsafe driving behavior is observed on camera, the driver is coached that this is a risky thing. She realizes that her behavior is being seen, it is being measured and it matters. Not surprisingly, once this is realized, that behavior will stop—so long as the person coaching the driver continues to reinforce that it matters and that they care about the behavior being exhibited.

Another thing that happens, over time, is that once drivers get the feel of the amount of G-force it takes to trigger the video recorder to save the event, they learn how to "trick" the system. As it was so eloquently described in our previous chapter, drivers do that by not speeding, tailgating, swerving, following too closely or engaging in any other activity that will cause them to react in an abrupt fashion. And what happens when they behave this way? They drive in a safe and responsible manner. That saves them, and their companies, 50 percent or more in both frequency and severity of crashes.

Fleet or passenger vehicle. Younger driver or older driver. Male or female. Black or white. Christian or Muslim or Jew. It doesn't matter. The result is the same. Behavior changes.

Even in teenagers.

## Starting Young

Teenagers are the most susceptible to collisions with five times the number of incidents as other drivers. In April 2007, the WHO announced that "road traffic crashes are the leading cause of death among young people between 10 and 24 years." The report, *Youth and Road Safety*, states that nearly 400,000 young people under the age of twenty-five are killed in road traffic crashes every year. Millions more are injured or disabled." But, they can be coached and their driving skills improved.

For instance, teen drivers participating in the Teen Safe Driver Program (TSDP) had 70 percent fewer at-fault crashes and 75 percent fewer at-fault injury crashes than would have been expected based on national driving statistics. In addition, there was an average 80 percent reduction in driving risk scores during the first sixteen weeks of program participation.

The TSDP was launched in March 2007 by American Family Insurance (AFI). AFI made the program available, at no charge, to its insured families in three states (Indiana, Wisconsin and Minnesota). Consumers were encouraged to enroll in the program at TeenSafeDriver.com.

The statistics here are so overwhelming that I have to share them with you. I'm sure you'll be as blown away by the results as I was when I saw them. In a nutshell, the results showed a 70 percent decrease in the frequency and severity of high-risk driving events.

As of August 30, 2007, there were 600 teens who had driven a total of 1,620 months (135 participant years) in the TSDP. Studies aligned with data from the National Household Travel Survey shows a consistent estimate of 10,000 miles per year. At that rate, these teens had driven a total of 1.3 million miles during this initial reporting period.

Results were collected in two ways—driving risk score and crashes. A risk score for each driving event was assigned by driving risk analysts, and the cumulative score by week was plotted by driver. A combined score by week was then created for all drivers. This combined score showed an 80 percent reduction from twenty-three points in weeks one and two, to less than four points in weeks sixteen and seventeen.

Crashes were reported by the driving risk analysts who saw videos of the events and by families calling or e-mailing to report them. Based on these inputs, the crashes were categorized as "at fault" and "no fault"

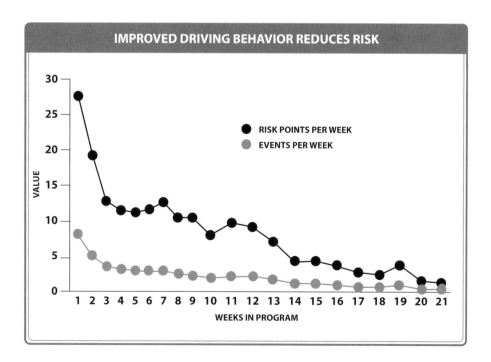

as well as "reportable" (injuries or property damage over $1,000) and its subset "injury" crashes.

We can make general comparisons with crash data published by the IIHS and NHTSA. Although there is some amount of selection bias because American Family doesn't insure high-risk drivers, the difference in population means is so great, and the change in driving risk scores for the same driver over a short time is so dramatic, this selection bias is small compared with the reduction in crash frequency produced by the TSD program.

The paper, *Crashes of Novice Teenage Drivers: Characteristics and Contributing Factors* by Braitman et al (IIHS February 2007) lists twenty-six police-reported crashes per million miles traveled for sixteen-year-olds as a group, and twenty-one crashes per million miles for seventeen-year-olds (average twenty-four crashes per million miles). It also points out that teen drivers are at fault about 75 percent of the time.[4]

These numbers are similar to those reported by Allan Williams in his 2003 paper, *Teenage Drivers: Patterns of Risk* (IIHS) based on the National Automotive Sampling System/General Estimates System. In this paper, Williams reported a national probability sample of police-reported crashes in 1995 of thirty-five crashes per million miles for sixteen-year-olds and twenty for seventeen-year-olds. The paper also listed crashes by age group, showing sixteen-year-olds are nine times more likely to crash than those aged forty to sixty-nine, and the sixteen-to seventeen-year-old group is five times more likely to crash than the average of all drivers.[5]

NHTSA data for 2005 shows an average injury rate for all drivers of 0.91 per million miles traveled. Using the 5x ratio again, we would expect young drivers sixteen to seventeen years old to have had 4.5 injury crashes per million miles of driving.

While this is not a study with a directly comparable control group, the treatment group is large and spread out enough, and the differences between population means is so large, that we can draw meaningful conclusions from these initial results.

While data was not available at the time of this report to predict the exact effectiveness of this program at reducing crashes in large populations of teen drivers, early indicators were compelling. So compelling, in fact, AFI expanded the program to their eighteen-state territory within nine months of their initial launch.

| CRASHES OF NOVICE TEENAGE DRIVERS | | | | | |
|---|---|---|---|---|---|
| | Expected Total | Actual Total | Expected At Fault | Actual At Fault | Reduction |
| Reportable Crashes | 31 | 19 | 23 | 6 | 74% |
| Injury Accidents | 5 | 2 | 4 | 1 | 75% |

## Watch the Road

The best part about all this data and these statistics is that the number of crashes can be reduced in *both* teenagers and adults. We know the reason for crashes, and we know how to prevent them. It's now a matter of getting drivers to pay attention to those reasons and to do something about them.

The leading factor in most crashes? Driver inattention. According to a landmark research report released by NHTSA and the Virginia Tech Transportation Institute (VTTI) in mid-2006, "Nearly 80 percent of crashes and 65 percent of near-crashes involved some form of driver inattention within three seconds before the event. Primary causes of inattention are distracting activities, such as cell phone use and drowsiness." If only people would pay attention, I wouldn't need to report these facts:

- Drowsiness is a significant problem that increases a driver's risk of a crash or near-crash by at least a factor of four.
- The most common distraction for drivers is the use of cell phones.
- Reaching for a moving object increased the risk of a crash or near-crash by nine times.
- Drivers who engage frequently in distracting activities are more likely to be involved in an inattention-related crash or near-crash.

But, no matter how many times someone reads these figures, they always say, "It's not me; it's the other guy. I always get plenty of sleep. I only use my cell phone in the car for emergencies. I always keep my hands (both of 'em) on the wheel."

If only they'd look in the mirror and see themselves. Yes, the rear-view mirror. The one they look in every day. If only they'd realize that it's not always the other guy. Sometimes it's them. It's me. And yes, it's you. There are times when we are all at fault … and at risk.

In the end, you'll still pay taxes and someday you will die, but I want to make sure that doesn't happen in an automobile crash through your own or others' distracted—or risky—behavior.

---

[1] Wards Motor Vehicle Facts & Figures, 1999

[2] Dictionary.com

[3] CNN Money.com, Lesson 22, Auto Insurance

[4] Braitman KA; Kirley BB; McCartt AT; Chaudhary NK. 2007. Crashes of novice teenage drivers: characteristics and contributing factors. Insurance Institute for Highway Safety.

[5] Williams, AF. 2003. Teenage drivers: patterns of risk. Journal of Safety Reseach 34: 5–15.

## Chapter 14

# The Controversy between Privacy and Safety

Which side of the debate are you on? Privacy or safety? My bet is that you're probably on the side of privacy—especially when it is your own we are debating.

However, you might be on the side of safety, as it is a little like motherhood, apple pie and saving the planet. So long as it doesn't inconvenience or threaten you, everyone is for it.

There is real science behind this position. It makes sense and is a normal, rational thing for a human being to feel. Privacy is equated to freedom and is really part of the base in Abraham Maslow's famous "Hierarchy of Needs:"

Abraham Maslow's Hierarchy of Needs is often depicted as a pyramid (next page) consisting of five levels: the four lower levels are grouped together as *deficit needs* associated with:

- Physiological needs (hunger, thirst, sleep, etc.)
- Safety (reflecting man's desire for protection against danger or deprivation)

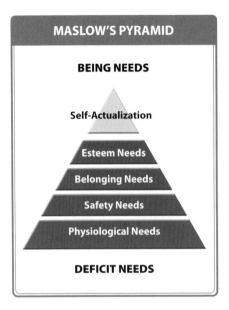

- Love or belonging to (functions of man's gregariousness and his desire to belong to a group, to give and receive friendship and to associate happily with people)
- Esteem (the desire for self-esteem and self respect, which are affected by a person's standing reputation and his need for recognition and appreciation

The top level is termed *being needs* associated with self-actualization or a desire for self-fulfillment, which is an urge by individuals for self-development, creativity and job satisfaction.

*Deficit needs* must be met first. Once these are met, seeking to satisfy *being needs* drives personal growth. The higher needs in this hierarchy only come into focus when the lower needs in the pyramid are satisfied. So, for instance, physiological needs must be met prior to safety needs and safety needs must be met prior to belonging needs. Once an individual has moved upward to the next level, needs in the lower level will no longer be prioritized. However, if a lower set of needs is no longer being met, the individual will temporarily re-prioritize those needs by focusing attention on the unfulfilled needs. This hierarchy of needs appeared in Maslow's 1945 paper, *A Theory of Human Motivation,* and is still used today in a variety of industries.

Just as we need air, food, water and shelter, privacy—although not a level on Maslow's pyramid—is part of that cocoon of protection. We don't want to be controlled or badgered to do something against our will or our best survival interests. Privacy helps us with our need to be free of external constraints and influences that may or may not be aligned with our very own survival. We need it. We want it. But, is it an inalienable right?

In fact, privacy is not even mentioned in the U.S. Constitution. The fourteenth amendment is often cited as the amendment that protects what Justice Louis Brandeis called the "right to be left alone," but it appears that a fair amount of interpretation has to be allowed to come to the conclusion that it inherently protects our privacy. And, although the first, fourth and fifth amendments are also occasionally referred to in privacy rights discussions, they don't grant it as an inalienable right.

Of course, the tenth amendment explicitly grants authority to the individual states for any power not delegated to the United States Congress or prohibited explicitly in the Constitution of the United States. So, there may very well be provisions protecting privacy in state constitutions or state laws. There are also a number of statutes and regulations at both the federal and state levels based, in part, on the inferred right of privacy. Unfortunately, privacy, and the protection of sensitive or personal information, seems to be legislated on an industry-by-industry basis.

## Privacy Defined

But, what is privacy? Privacy is …

> "… the expectation that confidential personal information disclosed in a private place will not be disclosed to third parties, when that disclosure would cause either embarrassment or emotional distress to a person of reasonable sensitivities. *Information* is interpreted broadly to include facts, images (e.g., photographs, videotapes), and disparaging opinions."[1]

The right of privacy is restricted to individuals who are in a place that a person would reasonably expect to be private (e.g., home, hotel room, telephone booth). There is no protection for information that either is a matter of public record or the victim voluntarily disclosed in a public place. People should be protected by privacy when they "believe that the conversation is private and cannot be heard by others who are acting in a lawful manner."[2]

But do we still have a right to privacy as we pursue happiness? What if it puts us in harm's way, or puts those around us in harm's way? Don't we need some boundaries and safety measures to protect ourselves and others?

## What about Safety?

Safety would seem to be an even more obvious choice for an individual to make—even at the expense of privacy. It is absolutely more basic and more directly specific to Maslow's Hierarchy of Needs. In fact, it is a level on his pyramid. But, what is safety? And are we willing to give up safety for privacy and vice versa?

Safety is...

> ... the state of being "safe" (from French *sauf*), the condition of being protected against physical, social, spiritual, financial, political, emotional, occupational, psychological, educational or other types or consequences of failure, damage, error, accidents, harm or any other event that could be considered non-desirable. It's important to realize that safety is relative. Eliminating all risk, if even possible, would be extremely difficult and very expensive. A safe situation is one where risks of injury or property damage are low and manageable.[3]

In the early days after the Twin Towers were knocked down, we overwhelmingly ceded control over our own lives and certainly our privacy in favor of our personal safety. We now accept the fact that we will take off our shoes and coats and submit to any, and all, manor of search when we go to the airport. The expectation is that we will board an airplane which will safely and uneventfully arrive at its destination. All as a result of the safety precautions we took prior to boarding.

Examples of our society trading freedoms for safety are abundant. But now, as the pendulum swings back from whence it came, as it always does, questions emerge as to how safe are these subtle surrenders of privacy really making us? And, are we still—or were we ever—really under potential assault in the first place?

Now then, assuming the posture of safety being a more direct determinant of our survival than privacy, who wouldn't want to be as safe as is reasonable?

But, as it turns out ...

## Safe Is Not Simple

Safe can be smothering. It can impede our freedoms. It can make us do, or not do, things which might give us pleasure. In fact, in some cases, things that might give us immediate pleasure.

On one level, safety is freedom from risk. But most of us are not great at assessing risk. As Thornton Wilder said, "When you're safe at home you wish you were having an adventure; when you're having an adventure you wish you were safe at home."

An example would be mountain climbing. In order to scale the sheer side of a mountain by finding cracks and crevices with which to anchor and leverage oneself up, inch by inch and foot by foot, to ultimately perch at the top and conquer the mountain, seems to be a very high risk to most of us. To those who do it and get good at it, it gives purpose and meaning to life. To others, it's not a matter of whether they're crazy, but rather, how crazy are they to do it?

One of my own personal heroes was Steve Irwin, The Crocodile Hunter, who was so in tune with nature and so passionate about all of the creatures with whom he interacted, that you could tell he was truly one with nature. To some, it may have seemed that he thrived on risky or unsafe behavior. Sadly, it was the barb of a normally docile stingray that ultimately led to his untimely demise, but I can't imagine him living his life any differently. His purpose and his passion may have seemed risky to some, but I'm pretty certain he would have argued against that point of view to the day he died. As evidenced in one of his quotes, "I probably don't show fear, but I suffer from fear like everyone else. I have no fear of losing my life—if I have to save a koala or a crocodile or a kangaroo or a snake, mate, I will save it."

But what is safe and what is unsafe behavior is a debatable subject. And, what may be risky for someone may be prudent and rational for others.

## Patterns or Habits. Both Lead to Incidents.

One could rightfully argue that driving is among the most dangerous things we can undertake on a daily basis. In fact, far more people die in traffic collisions every year than they do in aviation mishaps. As we discussed earlier, close to 43,000 people die every year on our

U.S. highways with nearly three times that many perishing on the roads in the European Community.

Unfortunately, having access to the world's largest repository of risky driving behavior heightens my awareness to various truths and patterns.

Almost, without exception, there are avoidable patterns of behavior that can be intercepted and broken before they become what we all don't want to even think about. Patterns that become habits. Patterns we don't even recognize as patterns: tailgating, reaching for that sip of hot coffee, text messaging and eating that missed breakfast while driving with our knees. In general, trading the short-term pleasures of food or rushing to not be late for a meeting, for the increased risk of snuffing out our very existence in an instant.

## Safety and Privacy. Not Safety versus Privacy.

The very essence of our human nature is to seek food and shelter in the here and now, while potentially trading off better choices for the longer term future. When we do this while driving, we are introducing another level of risk that is far greater than we can comprehend. That is where privacy can actually benefit drivers in an almost oxymoronic manner. What happens, for instance, if you are observed and then coached (on an exception-only basis), every time you do something that can result in your loss of life or limb? Or even when you do something that threatens your very survival as an individual and, therefore, the species in general? You are using the tool of privacy to help you obtain the safety (security) that is driving your core behavior in the first place.

So what if your privacy was open to scrutiny each time … but only when you did something that could potentially snuff out your very existence? And the existence of those around you?

Would that be a loss of a few seconds of privacy? Or would it be a guardian angel or perhaps, a conscience, keeping you focused, and in the moment, while you navigate the dangerous art of driving?

If you really knew the dangers awaiting you every time you turned on the ignition key, and could be kept safe from patterns of potential lethal destruction, the privacy versus safety debate would no longer be a debate. One now becomes the servant to the master. One becomes in control of both—safety and privacy. The best part is that even though you need both, you also deserve both. And as a normal functioning human being, your nature will drive you to obtain both, without you even realizing it.

You can have your cake and eat it, too. Just not while you are driving. But if you do, a DRM (with an exception-based video event recorder) will help keep you from doing your best bug-on-the-windshield impersonation. It'll take a few precious seconds of your past behavior and turn them into years of living, laughing and loving with those who don't know you as, or think of you as, a number or a statistic. In other words, a safer, more secure life will cost you a few minutes of privacy. It's a price most people are willing to pay.

---

[1] Dr. Ronald B. Standler, 1997

[2] Am.Jur.2d *Telecommunications* § 209 (1974)

[3] Wikipedia

## Chapter 15

# Luck, Plain Luck

Whenever I think of the classic movie, *A Christmas Story*, the first thing that comes to mind is not the father swearing at the blinkety-blank furnace in the basement, or the "major prize" he won in the form of the leg lamp.

It's a phrase. You know which one it is. You know it because it is an admonishment we all heard as kids and now, as confirmation that we really are turning into our own parents, we say it to our kids, too.

"You'll shoot your eye out!"

Now tell me. How many one-eyed children have you ever encountered? (Before you start writing me, yes, I know it does actually happen.)

But, how does such a ubiquitous and well-meaning parental phrase become so universally ignored and reviled by children of all ages? I argue that it's because the recipient of this rebuke instinctively processes the danger, the benefits and the available choices, while weighing the risk/reward scenarios (safe versus fun!), to come up with what is believed to be the appropriate behavior. Sort of sounds like weighing the privacy versus safety scenario, doesn't it?

In other words, the potential of losing an eye from engaging in hedonistic behavior is not certain and it's never happened to us before. More importantly, if we were to lose that eye, that is definitely further in the future than is the enjoyment of the risky behavior right now.

So, translated beyond childhood to the world at large, we as a society do suffer greatly by the same behavioral phenomenon that propels Ralphie to take those risks with his eyes. We weigh the risks, figure they are not real and, like Ralphie, take the riskier route.

## From Childhood to Adulthood

Now think about how you behave when you are behind the wheel of your car—or worse yet, think about how that other son of a BB-gun behaves when he is pretending he can drive! Of course, it's always the other guy who is the irresponsible risk-taker. He's the one who continually cuts people off, changes lanes and thinks the shoulder is his own personal driving lane. We, on the other hand, are mature, responsible drivers who have never been in a crash, have great reflexes, amazing instincts, and are … pure and simple … very good drivers. We've seen it all, done it all, and like Ralphie, we've never even come close to putting our proverbial eye out.

In fact, we're so good, we can eat, drink, read our e-mail, text message, sing, contemplate, stare, tailgate, navigate and investigate all while we are driving. All with confidence, baby! Never had a crash, never had a ticket. Yeah, we're good! We're very good.

In actuality, we're just lucky. Very lucky!

Except when we're not.

As you've read earlier, every year about 43,000 of us will have our luck run out in the United States alone. That's not *some* luck running out, that's all of it. We're not talking eye injuries here. We're talking about 43,000 meeting the grim reaper. The pale rider. The angel of death.

What's hard to understand is that the very same behaviors that are causing all of this death and destruction are happening all of the time. That ratio of 300 unsafe or risky driving behaviors to every twenty-nine accidents that we discussed before seems to continue, with everyone oblivious to it.

Is it because we don't see the consequences of that unsafe behavior on a daily basis? Or is it that it only seems to happen to the other guy, rather than to us? Or—unfortunately—is it because of pure, unadulterated bad luck that, this one time, the result of our doing the same things we always do in our cars every day, happened to result in one vehicle actually hitting someone or something—rather than just hitting thin air?

Same behavior, different result.

## Luck, Just Plain Luck

That's all it is. Luck, just plain luck.

What's even worse is that we are seduced by previous good fortune into thinking that we really are the superior driver because we've never had a ticket or a collision. We think we are in control. However, the difference is us. We become even more confident, which is being reinforced by even more luck. Until, that is, that one day arrives when we are either so outrageously over-confident or we are just not lucky. That one day when the consequences for us, for others, their respected loved ones and for the people who insure them, are devastating and expensive.

Let's go back to the basics for a minute. Let's go back to that fateful day when your driver's license examiner watched every move you made and kept you from becoming cocky and over-confident. What if you went back to behaving behind the wheel as if it really mattered? What if you went back to behaving behind the wheel as if it were being measured and you were held accountable for risky behaviors and coached out of them before you became—or caused—someone else to become a statistic? What if you simply started to pay attention to this daily routine as if each and every moment behind the wheel could mean the difference between life and death? Between keeping the lights burning bright and turning them out forever?

That's what a DRM program can do for you. And that's why so many drivers have come to rely on this type of program. The exception-based video event recorder silently sits there, behind the rearview mirror, monitoring and protecting. If nothing significant happens, it just keeps on rolling and writing over itself. If, however, something does happen, the recorder is there to report the truth.

This type of constant companion—or buddy—has reduced incidents and collisions by more than 50 percent. And, in the case of teenage drivers, it's already reduced incidents and collisions by 70 percent.

So while I won't admonish you that "you'll shoot your eye out," I will tell you, you are an incident waiting to happen. And someday, your luck *will* run out. Just remember one thing … it doesn't have to be that way.

## Chapter 16

# Driving under the Influence

I come from a long line of distinguished drunks.

I can remember as a kid, before the days of seat belts and open container laws, my father taking me out for a not-so-typical father-son bonding event. To this day, I am an excellent shuffle-board bowler, as I spent hours perfecting this skill in his favorite neighborhood bar. After the appropriate time drinking and bowling, we'd put the top down on the convertible and go for a joy ride with Dad driving fast on old back highways. I remember those steep, curvy country roads with dips in them and me standing at the right time to let the dips fling me backward into the back seat. I remember the roller coaster feeling that gave my stomach. It was the same tingly feeling as the tilt-a-whirl at the traveling carnival.

At the tender age of twelve, I took my turn at the wheel and began driving my Dad's 1964 Thunderbird. Now he could enjoy the ride without the burden of supposedly having to be in control of the vehicle. The roads were back country and gravel. But I'm sure the joy of popping that beer can and feeling the sun on his face, the wind in his hair and the buzz in his head while making his son a man early in life, had to be one that far outperformed those thrills modern day dads get by doing laundry, washing dishes and coaching their kids' baseball teams. Ah, for the good old days.

It seems strange today to reflect on the way things used to be. The days before cell phones, BlackBerrys, DVDs, satellite radio, the Internet and all the other things that date us. My kids don't even believe me (but they do laugh) when I tell them of days gone by. Of days when you had to wait until one of three broadcast stations decided to play *It's a Wonderful Life* or *The Wizard of Oz*. Better yet, remember when you had to wait until your birthday for those jeans you just had to have, instead of having to wait just until the weekend?

It seems crazy and irresponsible to think that a father would take his little boy to the bar for his recreation. It's even crazier when you think that cars didn't even have seat belts or that you could literally drink and drive simultaneously back then. Now that was an accident waiting to happen!

My mother, at least, was wise enough to know that she couldn't, or shouldn't, be driving. She had plenty of trouble just getting herself from point A to point B on foot or on the bus without getting into a verbal confrontation with some relative or stranger. I now realize, in retrospect, that her ability to confront anyone or anything was fueled by liquid courage.

## Freedom. Pure and Simple.

I, and most of the kids I knew, had one pair of blue jeans and they were several inches too long so we could grow into them. When we first got them, they were like wearing iron until we finally broke them in. Sound familiar? So while faded or ripped jeans are a fashion statement today, yesterday they were merely a badge of honor. You wore them down to be that comfortable old friend that might be faded or ripped, but that finally fit you and gave you the freedom to walk and run without chafing.

Freedom was the driving force. Freedom from discomfort. Freedom from the rigidity of what your parents, neighbors, clergy and teachers thought was the proper way for you to think, act and feel.

Back in the '60s when I was growing up, we weren't fighting against the terrorists for our freedom as we are today. We weren't fighting against wire-tapping, invasive telemarketers, identity theft or even water boarding. We just wanted to be free on an individual basis to go where we wanted, when we wanted, to do what we wanted, with whomever we wanted, dressed the way we wanted with our hair grown as long as we wanted. Freedom. Pure and simple.

The entire backlash under the guise of freedom was our collective response to an overly controlled, overly structured environment that manifested itself in protests, drugs, burnt flags, drop outs, communes and a number of other escape mechanisms.

Upon reflection, I think that desire to be free and to escape the rigidity of the expectations of their bosses, parents and other societal influences was what my own parents were seeking when they sought to escape through alcohol. And they were just two in a world of alcoholics. It is estimated that approximately 8 percent of American adults are abusers of alcohol at any given time. In fact, 100,000 Americans die each year of alcohol-related causes.[1] My parents were part of those statistics.

In my own case, after witnessing, first hand, the destructive forces of alcohol upon most of my family, I wanted no part of that particular brand of freedom. I also wasn't interested in the drug-induced serenity of the commune-living counter-culture movement. So although I missed out on that whole free love scene that John and Yoko exemplified in their famous bed interviews, I was happy to achieve my freedoms by virtue of my automobile. After all, thanks to my father's superior parenting wisdom, I had already been driving for over four years by the time I was eligible to take my first driver's license test.

## The Key to Freedom

As a reasonably happy teenager who didn't yet know how to delve into the meaning of life, define freedom, or rebel against my government, school or church, I also didn't know that the unexamined life was not worth living. Because of this, I blithely went through those tumultuous years obsessing about cars, girls and sports—not necessarily in that order.

Through it all, one obsession remained front and center—the car. The car was the key to my freedom. If I could only get that license and that car!

I could go where there were better people in better neighborhoods with better sports teams. I could go where they might have cuter girls who might see me for the great potential I had instead of the insecure and unworldly kid that I was and still am. I could go where I wanted, when I wanted, and with whom I wanted.

So, my father and I forged an unholy alliance. Suddenly we enjoyed one another's company even more than ever. I had a driver's permit, he was an adult (well, legally), we had a car, and I could drive him from bar to bar and anywhere else either of us could think to go. But only as long as this license-bearing adult sat in the front seat next to me supervising me. Because that was the law.

There was, however, one little itty bitty, miniscule, pint-sized, tiny technical problem with this particular piece of logic of which I was keenly aware. I believe today, reflecting back on that time, it's what made me a much better driver.

This tiny little problem was that, although my dad was an adult sitting next to me and I was driving his car using my hard fought driver's permit, HE DIDN'T HAVE A VALID LICENSE! This vicious cycle that had been a part of my entire life was finally catching up with me … and with him.

You see, he had been caught driving under the influence so many times that he had lost his license, and just didn't bother to get one anymore. Back then, they didn't lock you up and throw away the key for drunk driving. So he remained out on the roads doing what he couldn't help himself from doing, but driving nonetheless! He considered needing a license to drive a government intrusion. So, if he didn't have one of their licenses, well damn them to hell anyway. It wasn't going to stop him.

But, could it stop me? In addition to being the responsible one of the two of us at the tender young age of fifteen and a half, there were several other problems to consider. One that continually presented itself during this unfortunate period was that I certainly did not want to be the one responsible for him getting caught, once again, driving under the influence. I knew that the result of his being caught would be likely losing his job as a salesman, paying another fine he couldn't afford and being thrown in jail—again. Especially if he were caught sitting next to me "supervising" my permit-enabled driving. As a consequence, I drove carefully—very carefully—and watched for police, kids on bikes or other odd drivers' behaviors to protect my dad. I also did it to keep driving so I could test for my own license as soon as I was legal to do so (sixteen in Illinois at the time).

It was stressful and I knew it was risky. But I wanted to drive to attain that freedom I so eagerly craved. I undertook the only way I knew how to achieve my goals. I drove carefully. Very carefully.

## Driving Under My Own Influence

I drove carefully and became a competent driver because someone was always watching, even if that someone (Dad) didn't have a valid driver's license. I didn't have the luxury of making a mistake because Dad's sad life and livelihood were also at stake. I drove carefully out of a sense of responsibility to him. I didn't take chances due to my genuine love and caring for the man who, with all his faults, did everything in the world he could for me except the one obvious thing I have come to realize that he couldn't do—stop drinking.

However, driving with an adult under a learner's permit when that adult didn't actually possess a valid driver's license was one thing. Turning sixteen and going to the DMV to get my own license was quite another.

That detail, I knew, we couldn't dodge. It kept me scheming and conniving so I could finally take that damn test and get my own license. If you remember, from an earlier chapter, we ultimately convinced one of Dad's casual friends to drive me down to the DMV shortly (very shortly) after my sixteenth birthday.

Incredibly, I don't even remember that man's name, but I do remember the circumstances. I was so intensely focused upon getting my first license that I somehow convinced that poor man to take me to the DMV during a classic January Chicago snowstorm! He probably also knew my father and I were playing Russian roulette and wanted to get both of us out of harm's way and off of his back.

Nonetheless, I passed on my very first try. Mostly, I passed out of spite. I was so mad that I thought I'd blown the parallel parking part that I just completed the damn test with an overblown sense of confidence and abandon. That was, of course, another lesson for driving: If you drive defensively but with confidence, you can convince the man sitting next to you at the DMV that you know what you are doing and you will pass. Of course, I neglected to mention to him that I'd already been driving for four years. It didn't matter. I got what I wanted and what I needed.

ZITS © ZITS PARTNERSHIP, KING FEATURES SYNDICATE

## Lessons Learned—One, Two, Three ... and Four

There are several lessons for risky driving in this very personal story about my family's dynamics and driving under the influence.

**First of all,** people drink for a variety of reasons. Those with a real habitual problem do so because they can't stop and their pleasure/pain ordering has reconfigured in their brains. So, for my Dad, you can take the license away from the man, but you can't keep the drink or the wheel out of his hand. You have to inspect and monitor. If not, people will do whatever they have to in order to get their needs met.

**Secondly,** people actually do drive better and more cautiously if, and when, they think someone is watching, and if they know there will be consequences. It is a classic risk/reward thing. It works in business and it works in driving, too.

**Thirdly,** driving is a privilege and not a right. One has to be serious and somber about that privilege. We are sharing the public thoroughfares with one another and if you elect to drive while impaired, you might very well kill me or one of my loved ones. Although you don't think that will actually happen, because you can handle it, you are just wrong and you haven't done so thus far out of luck. Pure luck. Suffice it to say, I don't want to be there when your luck runs out. I see millions of risky driving events and combinations of behaviors, and I have seen it all. If I haven't seen it all, I guarantee you that I don't want to see the rest of it.

- Have you ever had to say goodbye forever to a child?
- Have you ever held a lifeless body one last time thinking why her, why not me and can't I please somehow wake up from this nightmare?

– Could you live with having inflicted that tragedy upon another family?

Of course not. You are a superior person with superior skills who would never let that happen. You're also someone who can handle it because you have been driving for fifty years, or you have been driving for one year, but you know you, and this just would never happen to, or with, you. You're confident. You're the best. And nothing has ever happened. Nothing ever will.

The **fourth lesson** is over-confidence. Those of us who think we are better than the average bear, who believe bad stuff only happens to the next guy, or who are so narcissistic that we just don't care, are truly accidents waiting to happen. Society cannot afford to let you do that so you have to be monitored and coached before you kill someone. It's not the actual money we cannot afford. It's the psychological impact your foolishness causes generations of humans who end up having to cope and compensate for their horrific losses in various ways. These actions can, in turn, perpetuate bad or dysfunctional behavior in many families yet to come.

## Forgiving but Not Forgetting

When I was very young, I thought my father was great. Despite his flaws, I thought he was smart and strong. I idolized him much the same way as all little boys do with their role models. I thought I wanted to grow up just like him. That is, until I noticed his right bicep. I don't remember how old I was when I noticed that scar, but I do remember asking him how he came about acquiring that experience. He somewhat awkwardly, and nervously, told me that he was involved in a rollover accident. He went on to say that although he had only this scar as a physical reminder of the incident, there was a woman killed in that crash. He didn't much want to elaborate upon that.

He told me he was driving. I don't know for sure, but I bet he was drunk.

Maybe that fatal crash was the demon that haunted him to drink the rest of his life. Which was cause and which was effect? I guess it really doesn't matter, as the behavior and its attendant problems and risks were there for all of us whose lives he touched; even strangers driving by on the other side of the roads he drove upon. It's just that they and

## TRUE OR FALSE?

**Alcohol-related driving accidents affect us every day. Test your knowledge by answering true or false to the following:**

- Alcohol-impaired driving will affect one in three Americans during their lifetimes.

- Alcohol-related motor vehicle crashes kill someone every 30 minutes.

- There were 13,470 deaths in 2006 involving drivers and motorcycle operators with blood alcohol levels over the legal limit in all states.

- In 2005, the number of people who died in alcohol-related motor vehicle crashes represented 39% of all traffic-related deaths.

- More than half of the 414 child passengers ages 14 and younger who died in alcohol-related crashes during 2005 were riding with the drinking driver.

- Of those children killed (above), fewer than 20% were properly restrained at the time of the crash.

- Each year, alcohol-related crashes in the United States cost about $51 billion.

- Male drivers involved in fatal motor vehicle crashes are almost twice as likely as female drivers to be intoxicated with a blood alcohol level concentration over the legal limit in all states.

- In 2005, 16% of drivers ages 16 to 20 who died in motor vehicle crashes had been drinking alcohol.

- In 2005, nearly 1.4 million drivers were arrested for driving under the influence of alcohol or narcotics.

**If you responded "True" to all of the above, you're correct. Sad, but true facts about our nation's roads and the people given the privilege to drive on them. Yes, people have the privilege to drive — not the right. But they also have the responsibility that comes with that privilege.**

society were unaware of the risks they were encountering because he was allowed to continue driving unmonitored and in whatever mental or physical state he happened to be in.

By the way, his brother also died in a rollover accident at age twenty-one. Two of his sisters died from alcoholism. His mother buried all six of her children. Some of that was unnecessary and avoidable.

One more lesson in all of this is that, unlike our counterparts in Europe, we in America decided to focus upon the vehicle for safety, rather than the human. Why? Because humans could not be trusted. Take seat belts, for instance. I guarantee you that when they were first introduced, I and my contemporaries, did not want to (and were not willing to) wear them. But, we got over it. It saved lives.

I see thousands of driving events every single day. Adults and kids (in particular) who are not monitored and given consequences, do what they want to do, when they want to do it, where they want to do it—just like we did in the '60s. Funny how things never change. But this just isn't funny.

Humans are humans and, mostly, they behave the same way and for similar reasons. That's why we have to focus on the human instead of just the car. It's the person who is driving—not the car—who is causing the crashes. As we discussed earlier, you get what you inspect and not what you expect.

---

[1] PlanetPsych.com 2006

True or False Sources:
1. NHTSA 2001a
2. NHTSA 2002a
3, 4, 5, 8, 9  NHTSA 2006
6. Quinlan KP, Brewer RD, Sleet DA, Dellinger AM. JAMA 2000
7. Blincoe L. Seay A, Zaloshnja E, Miller T, Romano E, Luchter S, Spicer R. NHTSA 2002
10. Department of Justice 2005

## Chapter 17

# Putting Safety in the Driver's Seat

Whenever I see someone driving erratically—either too slowly or drifting into and out of lanes as though they can't decide which lane to drive in—the very large majority of times there is a cell phone glued to the driver's ear. I always give them a very wide berth and shake my head in disgust as I pass them or otherwise maneuver to be outside of their potential zone of destruction.

It's obviously not the phone or the hand holding it. It's not even the art of speaking and driving at the same time, because, contrary to popular belief, many of us can walk and chew gum at the same time.

It is the fact that the task of driving has lost its priority in the person's mind and been replaced by the art of their conversation. They are *literally* no longer in the moment. As far as the act of driving is concerned, that driver has effectively lost his mind (to the conversation).

This can work as long as there are no unexpected emergencies on the road. The problem, however, is that they are not anticipating that other driver seemingly coming out of nowhere, or that kid darting out on a bicycle between the parked cars.

Simple things, like a construction road closure, are not register-ing with the driver engaged in the phone conversation. As a result, the driver often fails to recognize that he or she will eventually have to merge in or out of a lane so that other drivers can also pass through the remaining open lane. This can (and often does) enrage other drivers as an act of aggressive ill-will. In addition, our driver could be blocking other drivers from merging when the intent is not pernicious at all but, rather, just the manifestation of a disengaged mind.

And they're driving slower—forcing you and me to drive slower, too. A 2007 study by the University of Utah concludes that motorists talking on a cell phone (even with hands-free devices) crawl about 2 mph slower on commuter-clogged roads than people not on the phone. And they don't keep up with the flow of traffic. If you commute by car an hour a day, it could all add around twenty hours a year to your commute.

The study went on to find that drivers on cell phones are far more likely to stick behind a slow car and change lanes about twenty per-cent less often than drivers not on the phone. Cell phone drivers took about three percent longer to drive the same highly traffic-clogged route (and about two percent longer to drive a medium congested route) than people who were not on the phone. This is not too dis-similar from an earlier study that found that slower reaction times for drivers on the phone compared closely to reaction times of people legally drunk.[1]

Unfortunately, through my experience, I've seen thousands of videos where the driver attempts to make, take or engage in a call. The result? The driver usually rolls the vehicle over when hitting an uneven or soft shoulder or encounters some other unanticipated event. Most survive quite well and intact, but the look of first surprise and then the "Oh, shit" realization that it is too late to compensate for their inattention, is quite universal.

Interestingly, a law was passed in 2006 that prohibits the use of handheld mobile phones while driving in California. The law passed in 2006, but doesn't take effect until nearly two years later—July 2008. In those two years, how many lives will be lost because the law was not effective immediately? Using the CHP's own statistics from 2005, this two-year period equates to nearly 2,200 roadway crashes caused by hand-held cell phones. Remember Heinrich's pyramid from an earlier chapter? Those 2,200 unsafe acts equal 212 minor injuries and seven major injuries.

And, do those lawmakers think that a $20 fine for the first offense (and a $50 fine for subsequent offenses) will really make a difference? I'm sure that many people will receive fines and tickets for this offense and it will take many more years of wrangling and hot air to finally get a law passed with teeth in it, a law that will truly make a difference. According to the Governors' Highway Safety Association (2007):

- Five states (California, Connecticut, New Jersey, New York and Washington) and the District of Columbia have enacted jurisdiction-wide cell phone laws prohibiting driving while talking on handheld cell phones. Many other states ban cell phone use in specific situations.
- Seventeen states and the District of Columbia have special cell phone driving laws for novice drivers.
- School bus drivers in fourteen states and the District of Columbia are prohibited from all cell phone use when passengers are present, except for in emergencies.
- In May of 2007, Washington became the first state to ban driving while texting for all drivers. New Jersey followed suit in November and a few other states are considering similar measures.
- No state completely bans all types of cell phone use (handheld and hands-free) while driving.
- Some states, such as Utah and New Hampshire, treat cell phone use as a larger "distracted driving" issue.

Don't lawmakers and our government institutions realize that cell phones are one of the largest contributors to death on our highways? And, some of the most recent studies have shown that the distractions are the same, whether you are talking on a hands-free cell phone or not. Changes need to be made and they need to be made sooner rather than later. Before more lives are lost.

## Seat Belts

Have you ever seen that famous video where a cab driver falls asleep while driving on an almost empty four-lane highway in good weather on an early Saturday morning? The poor guy, made famous by television and YouTube, is driving along, without a seat belt, at around 40 miles per hour.

As you watch the video, you see his eyes start to close as he begins to drift off into his short dreamland vacation. Abruptly, the cab hits the soft shoulder of the road and he becomes startled and over-corrects. The car rolls over into the ditch, he gets thrown into the back seat because he is not wearing his seat belt, and the sheer look of terror, surprise and "Oh, shit!" is priceless.

The terrifying part is when you see his head slam through the rear window and the glass shattering throughout. The video ends and you are afraid he's dead. He isn't. Amazingly, he survived relatively intact, but you wouldn't know that if you had only seen the video.

The dramatic point to be made here is that this is the result of a relatively low-speed, non-contact roll over. All because he wasn't wearing his seat belt. None of this would have been news if he had. When you see, everyday, the thousands of scary examples we see everyday, it definitely makes you want to buckle up. Not surprisingly, it also has made many of us not want to drive at all!

So much can happen in an instant. Typically, as we have already discussed, it takes just three seconds. If you don't stay focused and in the moment—paying full attention to what you are doing—your world can (and will) change forever!

It's funny how I feel now when I get into a car and don't buckle up. Guilt comes to mind. Guilt is a funny thing. It plays on your mind years after you think it would. It's always there telling you what you know you should do but don't. But, you want to know what's worse? Your teenagers are not buckling up. And they don't feel guilty about it. They will tell you they are and you will believe them. You'll believe them because you know them and trust them.

But you know what? They aren't doing it. I know … *Your* kids are different, right? I thought mine were too.

It wasn't until December 1984 that the first seat belt law went into effect in the United States (more than ten years after Europe and Australia) and we still only have 81 percent compliance.[2]

Most people would think that all fifty states (plus the District of Columbia) have something as basic as a seat belt law to protect their citizens against "physical, financial, emotional, psychological consequences of damage, accidents or any other event considered non-desirable." Except for one state, they do. New Hampshire, whose motto is "Live Free or Die," does not have a seat belt law. In fact, New Hampshire residents still place their lives in someone else's hands each day they leave their driveways.

Bills requiring seat belt use have failed in New Hampshire for years. "We feel it's the most cost-effective and simplest means of cutting deaths and serious injuries in highway collisions," said Earl Sweeney, assistant commissioner of the New Hampshire Safety Department in 2007. "It seems like a simple act, to fasten a seat belt." But for many in rock-ribbed New Hampshire, buckling up and being told you have to buckle up are two very different things.

"It harkens to the libertarian 'don't tell me what to do' streak that characterizes much of our politics here," said the chairman

**NEW HAMPSHIRE**

**LIVE FREE OR DIE**

of the House transportation committee, Jim Ryan. Senator Robert J. Letourneau said that he thinks that citizens, especially children, should be educated about the benefits of seat belts, but that adults should not be required to use them. Requiring people to do things breeds resentment, Mr. Letourneau said, while encouragement does not. "We can't legislate common sense," he said. "The point of view to put these things into law, to change people's personal lifestyle, is not what I consider good policy. I trust our citizens to make those decisions for themselves."

This is fine thinking, except for the fact that in 2007, New Hampshire was one of the two states with the lowest rate of seat belt use in the country, 63.5 percent, according to the National Transportation Safety Board. In 2006, 77 percent of fatal crashes in New Hampshire involved occupants who were not wearing seat belts, according to the state's Safety Department. That means more than three quarters of every fatal collision involved someone not wearing a seat belt! Yet, the fine folks of

New Hampshire continue to allow their citizens to make this decision themselves, since the state can't legislate common sense.

This goes way beyond common sense. This is life and death. It's also a financial decision. In addition to the lives that would be saved, it's estimated that the state would save $48 million in medical costs by simply passing this bill. When people can't make a decision like this, then the state must insert itself and make the decision for them. Haven't they seen these statistics?

- Safety belts, when used properly, reduce the number of serious traffic injuries by 50 percent and fatalities by 60–70 percent.
- For every one percent increase in safety belt use, 172 lives and close to $100 million in annual injury and death costs can be saved.
- Safety belt use is one of the best defenses against the unpredictable actions of the drunk driver.
- A common cause of death and injury to children in motor vehicles is being crushed by adults who are not wearing safety belts. One out of four serious injuries to passengers is caused by occupants being thrown into each other.
- An estimated 80 percent of American children are immunized against contagious diseases, but less than 10 percent are properly restrained when riding in a motor vehicle.
- Motorists are twenty-five times more likely to be killed or seriously injured when they are "thrown clear" than when they remain inside their vehicle.[3]

Why can't New Hampshire's legislators get over their hubris and simply pass a law that will save lives each and every day? It's their civic duty. It's their responsibility.

## Child Restraints

I don't know how anyone in his or her right mind could ever harm a child. Particularly, on purpose … with forethought. It boggles my mind. Yet parents (so-called adults) do it every day. And, we're the ones who end up living with the tragedy.

I'm relieved to know that every state has a child restraint law. But, how may people abide by them? Maybe it will help you to know that about 350 children aged four to seven die in traffic crashes each year and about 50,000 are injured.[4] Half of those who do not die are not in any type of restraint. That's 25,000 kids.

As a result of these figures, Congress passed the Transportation Recall Enhancement, Accountability and Documentation Act (now that's a mouthful!), which directed the Department of Transportation to develop a five-year strategic plan to reduce deaths and injuries by 25 percent among four to seven year olds that were caused by failure to use booster seats. The latest results show that as many as 42 percent of children in this age range are not properly protected.

In one of our cases, a little girl was decapitated by a seat belt slung across her body. The problem was that the belt came over her neck because her parents did not put her in a booster seat first. You can bet that I think of nothing but *that* little girl, each and every time I buckle *my own* little girl into the back seat of my Jaguar.

Would parents proactively protect their children if they knew someone was watching? Do you think they'd think twice about not belting in their children or installing the car seat if they thought someone was keeping an eye on them? Think about what happens when a "Nannycam" is installed in a home. The difference in behavior is amazing once the nanny knows she is being watched. What if a similar device was packaged with car seats to help parents to both:

1. Remind them to install the car seat properly each time they ride with their child, and belt them in properly.
2. Ensure safer driving. Not only for themselves and the children in the car. But, also for those with whom they share the road.

In an ideal world (*my* world!), all infants and children in all vehicles should be covered by safety belt laws, child restraint laws or both. But, there are differences in the way the laws in various states are worded. The result is that many riders, particularly children, are covered by neither law. I'm happy that our lawmakers are finally eliminating these gaps by amending their child restraint and safety belt laws. But, they also need to make sure that our police can stop drivers to enforce the restraint laws covering older children. Laws without enforcement or penalties are like having no laws at all.

Yes, we need stronger laws. More importantly, we need less stupid parents.

## Air Bags

Although invented in 1951, air bags did not become standard equipment in automobiles until 1987—nearly forty years later! And to think that the first air bag, as standard equipment, was the Porsche 944 turbo. It was three years before (1984) that the U.S. government required cars produced five years after that (1989) to have driver's side air bags. Then, in 1998, dual front air bags were mandated by NHTSA. So, a technology that we take for granted today, took nearly fifty years to become mandatory and ubiquitous.

Fifty years! Think of the number of lives that could have been saved if this technology had been available sooner? According to NHTSA, since 1987, airbags have saved the lives of more than 4,800 people who otherwise may have died in vehicle crashes. Can we assume that an equal number of people would have been saved if they were mandatory twenty years earlier? Air bags save lives. Pure and simple.

Americans are supposed to be the leaders of the free world. The hotbed of change and innovation. We invent and innovate in America while the rest of the world watches and follows. Right?

Unfortunately, that may have been the case at one time. But when it takes us decades to adopt any meaningful change and adapt to the obvious meaningful benefits, the rest of the world is going to run right past our overly complacent society.

One Sunday, my teenage son approached me lamenting that he was bored and had nothing to do. I said he should go inside and study his math because that's what his future boss in India was probably doing on his Sunday. He looked at me dumbfounded and said, "Are you crazy? It's Sunday and I'm bored. I'm not going to go study math!" He then asked what had gotten into me and what was I thinking?

> If we, as a society, don't discipline ourselves to do the right things to make sure we are prepared to have a future, we either will have a poor quality future, or in the case of serious activities such as driving, we may not have a future at all!

Prevention is all about future and uncertain consequences. That's why no one is willing to spend time thinking about driver safety ... or fixing it.

It's obvious my son would rather complain about being bored, rather than undertake something constructive that would benefit him later. Similarly, drivers and operators of fleets prefer to wait until the crash happens and the damage is done rather than proactively intercede to prevent the crash in the first place.

So we know air bags save lives. And, we know that had they been mandated sooner, more lives would have been saved. But we also know that, with every yin, there's a yang. Since 1990, sixty-two adults and eighty-six children have reportedly died in crashes as a result of air bag injuries. Of the eighty-six children killed, investigations have proven that eighty-three of them were either not restrained, improperly restrained, or were in a rear-facing infant seat in front of a passenger air bag.[5]

So, do we remove air bags from automobiles because sixty-five people died over a seventeen-year period? No, we don't throw the baby out with the bathwater! We strive to improve technology, educate the public and reduce the deaths associated with air bags. The number of lives saved far exceeds those lost. We just need to continue to increase this difference.

## Beyond Cars

We need to work to continue improving technology, educate the public and change laws so we can reduce the number of incidents and deaths. For instance, it's been proven that an exception-based video event recorder can reduce incidents by over 50 percent. Yet, there are some laws on the books that don't permit the placement of a recorder on the window, behind the rear-view mirror.

This leads to my concern that there are laws currently on the books that may prevent carriers from keeping their drivers and our roads safe by not knowing their drivers' behavior. Laws written many years ago that did not allow for today's technology are hampering efforts to improve safety.

Everyone involved in the commercial vehicle industry needs to do everything in their power to ensure that we reduce the 4,995 large truck fatalities in 2006 to zero deaths in 2008 (and help to reduce the 43,000 total traffic fatalities to zero, as well). Talk to your Commercial Vehicle Safety Alliance representatives, your state legislators and everyone who can help make a difference. If we only reduced fatalities by 5 percent in 2007, we still would have had 4,476 fatalities. How many of those were *your* drivers?

More importantly, how many are future fatalities that could otherwise have been averted by just proactively breaking bad habits that *will* cause death and destruction if not eradicated at the source when drivers' luck runs out.

Families deserve mothers and fathers and sisters and brothers coming home safely each and every night. The emotional cost and havoc wreaked upon a family when victimized by a needless automotive fatality dwarfs the actual monetary cost.

As a society, we deserve more and should not accept less than striving to get to zero defects in this ongoing human tragedy.

---

[1] Drivers Using Cell Phones Can Put Commute on Hold/Study Finds they Slow Down, and you Pay the Price, Set Borenstein, AP, January 2008

[2] NHTSA Traffic Safety Facts, November 2006

[3] James Madison University, October 2004

[4] NHTSA Traffic Safety Facts, August 2007

[5] National Safety Council

## Chapter 18

# Despite Best Intentions ... Safety Takes a Back Seat in the Ride to America's Manifest Destiny

Many years ago, back when there were just the original thirteen colonies and people tended to stay within the regions in which they were deposited, some visionaries could see that the United States would eventually extend much further west.

Today, this seems quite obvious and natural. But imagine back then when people had barely accepted that the world was not flat. What they saw when they looked west was only dense forests, untamed wilderness and unreasonable natives who mistakenly thought this was their land.

Nonetheless, despite all obstacles, we did go west. And, despite the naysayers, we conquered all impediments we found in our way. This Manifest Destiny fueled a great economic growth over the last century as we knocked down forests, blasted through mountains, paved over old horse-drawn ruts in the road and then, with necessity being the mother of invention, we came to the realization that we quickly needed gas stations along these roads.

And so it began.

Where there was a road and a gas station, we also had to service tires that regularly blew out. While we were awaiting Gomer and Goober to fix our tires, we got hungry, so we had to have restaurants. Occasionally, the cousins couldn't fix our cars until they got a necessary part from Mount Pilot, so we had to sleep overnight. The result? Motels started to spring up.

As these necessities were being filled, we also had to have more workers for those businesses. This brought construction and concrete, so those suppliers built regional and then local depots. This then brought more jobs, which brought more people who needed to eat more. This, then, brought supermarkets. The cycle of economic growth and prosperity spun rapidly to many families' benefit.

We kept moving west. Acquiring, building, growing and becoming the economic powerhouse that made us the leader of—and the envy of—every other country. The dollar was the undisputed standard, and investments in housing, construction, petroleum and various other goods and services almost couldn't miss.

We quickly became a society enamored with our automobiles. They gave us the freedom to experience other cultures and towns. They allowed us to enjoy the best ice cream from this town, the best and biggest housing in that town, while driving to the highest paying jobs in the other town. This was our version of freedom. We met new people, saw new things and experienced that which we could never have in our own crumby little town. Our new mantra quickly became, "When I grow up, I'm gonna blow this popsicle stand and see the world!"

Jimmy Stewart in *It's A Wonderful Life* was forever trying to escape the shackles of the savings and loan in Bedford Falls for want of better, more exotic places far, far away. His yearning gave us hope and optimism that there was a better life out there. One yet to be discovered. One that kept us driving further and further westward.

## You're Not Alone

So, while the good times were rolling, more and more of us bought a car. But soon, one wasn't enough. Families began to buy two or even three vehicles. In fact, it's interesting to note that the average number of vehicles per household grew from 1.16 in 1969 to 1.90 in 2001 (even though the average number of persons per household declined from

3.16 to 2.58 in the same time period). This means that the distribution of vehicles per person per household doubled in thirty-two years.[1] With the increase in vehicles, our commutes became longer and the roads became more crowded.

To make traveling even more fun, some sadistic bastard came up with a novel approach to making this iron and concrete concoction even more challenging. By introducing bright orange cones to pinch off one lane, the three-mile back up over two lanes could now extend to eight miles over one lane! You haven't lived until you have experienced the hot summertime road construction traffic jam on Interstate 90 just west of Gary, Indiana, on the way to Chicago. I believe this to be the most congested place in the entire highway infrastructure in the United States. (And, if it isn't, I certainly don't want to discover the top spot on my own.) It's where minutes turn to hours and hours turn to days. For an extra added challenge, though, pick up a large super-sized iced tea just east of Gary. Go ahead and splurge by getting the wife and three kids one each, as well, so you can sit gridlocked in dead-stopped traffic surrounded by large trucks and metal all around you with no possible escape for hours on end. Talk about fun!

With so many people on the roads using this new fangled transportation, our federal and state governments eventually took note of all of the death and destruction on our highways. Despite the prosperity and feeling of freedom that the automobile brought, they took the bold action of requiring safety devices in vehicles— first seat belts and then air bags. We naturally rejected the notion of seat belts for several years. Yes, it was statistically proven to save lives, but it wrinkled our clothes and impeded our sense of freedom.

Over time and generations, however, we eventually acquiesced to wearing seat belts and, eventually, accepted air bags. In fact, some of us even began to feel wrong, or incomplete, when we didn't buckle up, or if our vehicle didn't have driver, passenger *and* side air bags. It took generations, governmental advertising campaigns, laws, tickets and yes, tragedies. But eventually, our hard heads came to accept that freedom and seat belts could co-exist.

Now we have car companies and other constituents, such as insurance companies, all supporting and promoting various safety devices on vehicles—back up cameras, lane departure warnings, global positioning systems for tracking, and driver risk management systems.

## I Repeat ... Accidents Are Not Accidents

The good news is that we are slowly starting to take a more responsible and serious posture toward safety. We no longer accept the theorem that accidents just happen. As we enjoy the benefits of more freedom, more economic expansion and endure congestion and ever-increasing fuel costs, I think we are coming to the realization that accidents are not accidents. They are always predictable and, therefore, preventable. Of course, we will invent many more distractions and diversions to make our driving task less arduous and tedious. Which, ironically, will make the driver even more dangerous. That's why we need to use the tools we have available to help people learn to drive safer.

With an ever-growing database of risky driving events, we are now at a point in this war on human tragedy to do the analysis and predict human behavior and potential collisions. Growing at a rate of more than 25,000 events a day, this database allows us the opportunity to see who's acting irresponsibly, predict who will act irresponsibly, and help coach people to drive safer and more responsibly.

We have to come to the level of maturity and acceptance where we focus our attention on one of the most deadly and costly by-products of all that freedom and prosperity: death and injury on our roads. Since the human is still in control of the vehicle, and since most incidents happen within a three-second window of inattention, we have to keep the driver focused upon the task at hand.

Think about it another way.

What if we were to let millions of people congregate in crowded spaces with loaded weapons? To make it even more fun, let's give them plenty of things to distract them so the shooting wouldn't be so tedious or mundane. We'll then mix it up so some have pistols, others have rifles, and still others have machine guns or even bazookas. Sound like a good idea? Didn't think so.

## The Price of Freedom

They say that there's a price for freedom and it doesn't come free. Our price is that 43,000 of us will perish each and every year.

But, crashes are preventable. We must have zero tolerance for them, and we must strive for zero defects. Just like the major, big-name companies, such as Dell and Motorola.

Yes, these companies make products that do not have life and death implications. But, they strive for zero defects because it makes their businesses stronger and more profitable. That's it! No safety issues. No life and death implications. Simply better business decisions. Why can't we, in the transportation industry, strive for the same with automobiles, trucks, transit and driving?

For us, as a society, it is well past the time when we *should* be acting responsibly toward one another and protecting life and property. It's time we *must*. As earlier chapters have detailed, the emotional, social and monetary costs are astronomical. That's why we, as individuals, have a great responsibility to act in a safe and responsible manner. We can't rely on our government to always tell us (or enforce) what to do. We will, as a point of human nature, always act in our own individual self-interest. However, this is not always in confluence with the best interests of the culture, as a whole, at any particular point in time. This is where the incidents occur.

The definition of insanity is doing the same thing over and over and expecting different results. We collectively go pigeon shooting every day. We don't change the way we drive. We kill one another every day. So the madness continues.

We may be slow, but we're not stupid. We can expect and demand better of one another and of ourselves. And we must. As we embark upon the next century of expansion and development, the situation will only worsen. It is time to act now. It's time to be both proactive and preventative. Another life lost needlessly is one too many and it is not acceptable anymore.

---

[1] U.S. Dept. of Transportation Federal Highway Administration

## Chapter 19

# Forward Technology, Forward Thinking

As technology moves forward to make our roads safer, so does the automotive industry. Take insurance, for instance.

Insurance is like many other commodities in our world marketplace. With information traveling at the speed of light and business models changing at the speed of thought, some bright and innovative insurance companies are now challenging the prevailing wisdom and suggesting that you should only pay for automotive insurance as, and when, you need it.

Today, insurance companies use a complicated and proprietary formula for underwriting their risk and pricing their automobile insurance products. Some of the ingredients are what your actual historical claims have been, along with where you park your car at night (crime rate), your credit score, how many shifts you work or miles you drive (exposure to risk), how expensive is your vehicle (replacement and parts cost) and probably some other weightings to which I'm not privy.

There is a movement (primarily coming out of Europe) that is referred to as Pay As You Drive™ (a trademark of Norwich Union Insurance). Some even call it "Insurance by the Mile." Following an extensive pilot in

---

## PAY AS YOU DRIVE (PAYD)

### Potential Benefits

- Potential cost-savings for responsible customers.

- Social and environmental benefits from more responsible and less unnecessary driving.

- Due to the 24/7 aspects of vehicle location, it enhances security — both personal security and vehicle security. The GPS technology could be used to trace the vehicle whereabouts following an accident, breakdown or theft.

- The same GPS technology can often be used to provide other (non insurance) benefits to consumers, e.g. satellite navigation.

- More choice for consumers on the type of car insurance available to buy.

- Social benefits from accessibility to affordable insurance for young drivers — rather than paying for irresponsible peers, young drivers pay for how they drive.

- Commercial benefits to the insurance company from better alignment of insurance with actual risk.

- Improved customer segmentation for the insurance company.

### Potential Drawbacks

- The system does not recognize actual risk.

- Charges would be very high for young drivers, especially at night, and as such would strongly discourage them from driving socially. In many areas, public transport is non-existent at night, and such high charges could have a strong negative impact on their quality of life.

- GPS tracking of vehicles, 24 hours a day, could be seen by many people as an unacceptable infringement on their right to privacy, although the devices do not necessarily beam live tracking data immediately back to the insurance company.

- The potential of PAYD systems for automated traffic law enforcement could result in a reduction of the use of human traffic police as has been reported since the widespread introduction of speed cameras. This could result in reduced detection of drunk driving and other dangerous offences.

– Wikipedia

---

October 2006, Norwich Union introduced this novel type of auto insurance. With Pay As You Drive (PAYD), a GPS receiver and mobile technology are placed in a car and different risk factors (time of day, distance, mileage) are directly monitored. Premiums are calculated dynamically, typically according to the amount you drive. The information is regularly transmitted directly back to the insurance company through a national network of satellites and data recorders. The result is that drivers using their vehicles at low-risk times of day, on low-risk roads or driving low mileage get a discount on their motor insurance premiums.

Insurance companies have always tried to differentiate and reward "safe" drivers, giving them lower premiums and/or a no-claims bonus. However, conventional differentiation is a reflection of past history rather than present patterns of behavior. This means that it may take a long time before safer (or more reckless) patterns of driving and changes in lifestyle feed through into premiums.

PAYD provides a much more immediate feedback loop to the driver, by changing the cost of insurance dynamically with a change of risk, which means drivers have a stronger incentive to adopt safer practices. For example, if a commuter switches to public transport or working at home, this immediately reduces the risk of rush-hour collisions. With PAYD, this reduction would be immediately reflected in the cost of car insurance for that month.

Oh, and there's one more benefit. If people pay for the actual miles they drive, and get rewarded for driving less with a smaller insurance bill, they'll drive less when they can. So, the driver wins. And so does our environment. Less driving, less gas, fewer emissions, less pollution, less global warming.

## The Way Things Used to Be

There are several industries that have adopted the digital world and the speed of the Internet in order to change the rules of the game. These changes make us look back at the way we (or our parents) used to do things in an almost comical manner. Take a moment and reflect as you read this true story …

One evening a grandson was talking to his grandmother about current events.

The grandson asked his grandmother what she thought about the shootings at schools, the computer age and just things in general. Grandma replied, "Well, let me think a minute …

"I was born before television, penicillin, polio shots, frozen foods, Xerox, contact lenses, Frisbees and the pill.

There was no radar, credit cards, laser beams or ball-point pens. Man had not invented pantyhose, air conditioners, dishwashers, clothes dryers and man hadn't yet walked on the moon.

"Your Grandfather and I got married first … and then lived together. Families had a father and a mother. Until I was twenty-five, I called every man older than me 'sir.' And after I turned twenty-five, I still called policemen and every man with a title 'sir.' We were before gay-rights, computer-dating, dual careers, daycare centers and group therapy. Our lives were governed by the Ten Commandments, good judgment and common sense. We were taught to know the difference between right and wrong and to stand up and take responsibility for our actions.

"Serving your country was a privilege; living in this country was a bigger privilege. We thought fast food was what people ate during Lent. Having a meaningful relationship meant getting along with your cousins. Draft dodgers were people who closed their front doors when the evening breeze started. Time-sharing meant time the family spent together in the evenings and weekends—not purchasing condominiums.

"We never heard of FM radios, tape decks, CDs, electric typewriters, yogurt or guys wearing earrings. We listened to the big bands, Jack Benny and the president's speeches on our radios. And I don't ever remember any kid blowing his brains out listening to Tommy Dorsey. If you saw anything with 'Made in Japan' on it, it was junk. Pizza Hut, McDonald's and instant coffee were unheard of.

"We had 5 and 10-cent stores where you could actually buy things for 5 and 10 cents. Ice-cream cones, phone calls, rides on a streetcar and a Pepsi were all a nickel. And if you didn't want to splurge, you could spend your nickel on enough stamps to mail one letter and two postcards. You could buy a new Chevy Coupe for $600 … but who could afford one? Too bad, because gas was 11 cents a gallon.

"In my day:

"'Grass' was mowed … 'Coke' was a cold drink … 'pot' was something your mother cooked in and 'rock music' was your grandmother's lullaby. 'Aids' were helpers in the principal's office … 'chip' meant a piece of wood … 'hardware' was found in a hardware store and 'software' wasn't even a word. And we were the last generation to actually believe that a lady needed a husband to have a baby."

No wonder people call us "old and confused" and say there is a generation gap. I bet you have an old lady in mind. But you are in for a shock—this woman would be only fifty-eight years old!

## The Way Things Need to Be

Within the last sixty years, the Internet and other new technologies have totally changed our society.

It may be time for the insurance industry to adopt some of these new technologies and provide pricing that rewards those of us who are responsible and avert risk, while appropriately pricing those of us who do reckless or even stupid things. Stupid is as stupid does.

PAYD insurance is an obvious next step evolution. Having a way to know how, when, where, what kind and how much risk you are exposing yourself to (and by extension, your insurance company), is a natural result that can save everybody a lot of time and a lot of money. It can also save the heartache and life disruption that comes from these stupid or reckless preventable acts.

But, PAYD is not the be-all and end-all. It's merely a step in the right direction. It is one more piece in the big puzzle to help ensure safer vehicles, safer roads and safer drivers. Enhancing PAYD is driver risk management. By observing driver behavior and coaching to improve it, we will make our roads safer. But we need to be forward thinking. That's why we created DrivingMeCrazyStories.com. A place for all forward thinkers to share their thoughts, ideas and stories. A place to observe, reflect and learn. But, most of all, a place to start making a difference.

It is time to change the way we do things and to harness the power of prevention. The place is here. The technology is available. And the world needed this intervention long ago. It is well past time for death to take a holiday.

# When the Inevitable Happens

## What to Do When the Inevitable Happens

No matter how well you drive, it's likely you'll be involved in a fender bender sometime, somewhere. Due to no fault of your own. So, here's a list of tips that will help make your collision less traumatic[1].

## DO:

(1)  Prepare by having a notepad, a few pens and a disposable camera in the glove compartment. Print out this article and store it to help you remember what to do.

Sketch the crash scene, noting all cars involved, roadways, direction of travel, skid marks and anything else to help your case. Write a description of what happened. Note any contributing factors like wet roads or blocked signs that couldn't be seen. Date, time and sign your notes. Photograph the scene.

(2)  Beware of scams. Some thieves will pretend to have a collision by bumping the rear of your car on an empty road. When you get out of the car to investigate, they rob you or steal your car. Drive to a populated place or police station before getting out of your car if things seem suspect.

(3) Copy down driver's license numbers and vehicle owner's registration information. Remember that the owner, i.e. the insured, might not be the driver. Find out the insurance company name and passengers' names along with the work and home telephone number of the driver.

(4) Record license plates and VINs (vehicle identification numbers) from the other cars. The VIN is located on the driver's side of the dashboard and can be seen through the windshield. This will help you later on if the driver happens to have stolen plates and a bogus registration card.

(5) Collect names, addresses and phone numbers of witnesses.

(6) Call the police if the crash is on a public roadway. They can help document your case and prove how it happened.

(7) Move your car and yourself off the highway after gathering all of your data/evidence. Standing in the street or waiting in your damaged car on the roadway can be dangerous. Turn on your flashers and put up warning triangles well in front of the crash to warn other drivers.

(8) Observe the other drivers' actions after the crash. If they are crawling under their car to inspect damage after a crash, then they don't have a serious injury. A photo of this wouldn't hurt your case.

(9) Control your temper. It is easier for the police to determine you are at fault if you are a raving hothead. You will be the one they remember two months from now in court. Stay cool.

(10) Get the names and badge numbers of police present. Each officer may have a different view of what the evidence was, and having contact with all of them might help your case.

(11) Get a copy of your claim file from your insurance company. Double check to make sure your claim is accurate. A mistake found today can save you from paying higher premiums in the future.

## DON'T:

(1)   Don't admit fault to anyone. Your words might be used against you later.

(2)   Never discuss how the collision happened. You don't want other drivers' versions of the car accident to influence yours, and you don't want something to slip out that makes you responsible.

(3)   Avoid moving your car until after you have other parties' license and vehicle registration information. Don't give the other driver a chance to drive off, leaving you with the problem.

(4)   Refuse to accept any roadside settlements. Often damage can be hidden and much greater than originally expected.

(5)   Don't let anyone pick your auto repair facility for you. You have the right, by law, to choose whichever auto repair shop you'd like, and your insurance must cover it. Ask your friends and neighbors for a reputable shop. Pick one that has been in business at least five years, preferably ten. You want a business that will be around if you have problems later.

For more tips, visit DrivingMeCrazyStories.com.

## AND ON THE LIGHTER SIDE...

**Accident insurance claim forms ask for a brief statement about how the accident happened. The combination of the finger pointing instinct and the small spaces provided on the forms can lead to some curiously phrased explanations.**

"A pedestrian hit me and went under my car."

"The other car collided with mine without giving warning of its intention."

"Coming home, I drove into the wrong house and collided with a tree I don't have."

"The pedestrian had no idea which direction to go, so I ran over him."

"I was taking my canary to the hospital. It got loose in the car and flew out the window. The next thing I saw was his rear end, and there was a crash."

"The indirect cause of this accident was a little guy in a small car with a big mouth."

"I had been shopping for plants all day and was on my way home. As I reached an intersection, a hedge sprung up, obscuring my vision."

"I was on the way to the doctor with rear end trouble when my universal joint gave way causing me to have an accident."

"When I could not avoid a collision, I stepped on the gas and crashed into the other car."

"In my attempt to kill a fly, I drove into a telephone pole."

"My car was legally parked as it backed into the other vehicle."

"The telephone pole was approaching fast. I was attempting to swerve out of its path when it struck my front end."

"A truck backed though my windshield and into my wife's face."

"I pulled away from the side of the road, glanced at my mother-in-law and headed over the embankment."

"An invisible car came out of nowhere, struck my vehicle and vanished."

– Rinkworks.com

---

[1] Auto Glass Across America, crackedwindshield.com

# Stories to Share

The following are stories I have collected over the years via the Internet, all in the public domain. I didn't make them up, and I believe most of them are meant to be true (if not absolutely true). Many are laugh-out-loud funny and remind us that, even with the best of intentions, things can go very wrong.

I hope you will take the time to enjoy these stories, think about the meaning behind them as they relate to this book and share them with your family, friends and colleagues.

And, don't forget to visit DrivingMeCrazyStories.com for more stories, videos and anecdotes. It's also the place for you to share your stories (true life and otherwise) as we build the momentum to end senseless "accidents" and make our roads safer for ourselves, our children and humanity.

One foggy night, a Cubs fan was heading north, and a Sox fan was driving south. While crossing a narrow bridge, they hit each other head-on, mangling both cars.

The Cubs fan manages to climb out of his car and survey the damage. He looks at his twisted car and says, "Man, I'm lucky to be alive!" Likewise, the Sox fan gets out of his car uninjured, he too feeling fortunate to have survived.

The Cubs fan walks over to the Sox fan and says, "Hey man, I think this is a sign that we should put away our differences and live as friends instead of rivals." The White Sox fan thinks a moment and says, "You know, you're absolutely right! We should be friends. In fact, I'm going to see if something else survived the wreck."

The Sox fan pops open his trunk and removes a full, undamaged bottle of Jack Daniels.

He says to the Cubs fan, "I think this is another sign. We should toast to our newfound friendship." The Cubs fan agrees and grabs the bottle. After sucking down half the bottle, he hands it back to the White Sox fan and says, "Your turn!"

The Sox fan calmly twists the cap back on the bottle, throws the bottle over the bridge into the river, and says, "Nah, I think I'll just wait for the cops to show up."

*And these classic stupid moves:*

A man who shoveled snow for an hour to clear a space for his car during a blizzard in Chicago returned with his vehicle to find a woman had taken the space. Understandably, he shot her.

An American teenager was in the hospital recovering from serious head wounds received from an oncoming train. When asked how he received the injuries, the lad told police that he was simply trying to see how close he could get his head to a moving train before he was hit.

When a man attempted to siphon gasoline from a motor home parked on a Seattle street, he got much more than he bargained for. Police arrived at the scene to find a very sick man curled up next to a motor home near spilled sewage. A police spokesman said that the man admitted to trying to steal gasoline and plugged his siphon hose into the motor home's sewage tank by mistake. The owner of the vehicle declined to press charges, saying that it was the best laugh he'd ever had.

From the county where drunk driving is considered a sport, comes this true story. Recently a routine police patrol parked outside a bar in Pittsburgh, Pennsylvania, after last call. The officer noticed a man leaving the bar so apparently intoxicated that he could barely walk.

The man stumbled around the parking lot for a few minutes, with the officer quietly observing. After what seemed an eternity in which he tried his keys on five different vehicles, the man managed to find his car and fall into it. He sat there for a few minutes as a number of other patrons left the bar and drove off.

Finally he started the car, switched the wipers on and off (it was a fine, dry summer night), flicked the blinkers on and off a couple of times, honked the horn and then switched on the lights. He moved the vehicle forward a few inches, reversed a little and then remained still for a few more minutes as some more of the other patrons' vehicles left. At last, when his was the only car left in the parking lot, he pulled out and drove slowly down the road.

The police officer, having waited patiently all this time, now started up his patrol car, put on the flashing lights, promptly pulled the man over and administered a breathalyzer test. To his amazement, the breathalyzer indicated no evidence that the man had consumed any alcohol at all!

Dumbfounded, the officer said, "I'll have to ask you to accompany me to the police station. This breathalyzer equipment must be broken."

"I doubt it," said the truly proud 'Burgh boy, "Tonight I'm the designated decoy."

---

*Sometimes you know that your children are really learning the safety lessons you demonstrate for them as in this next story:*

I was driving with my three young children one warm summer evening when a woman in the convertible ahead of us stood up and waved. She was stark naked! As I was reeling from the shock, I heard my five-year-old shout from the back seat, "Mom! That lady isn't wearing a seat belt!"

A car was driving very slowly down the highway. A state trooper pulls it over. "What have I done wrong, Officer?" the driver asks.

"You are going 26 mph on a major highway. There is a law against that," the officer says to the driver. "You must go at least 50 mph."

"But when I turned onto the highway, the sign said 26," the driver replies.

"Ha Ha Ha!" The officer laughs out loud. "That's because this is Interstate 26! The 26 isn't the speed limit."

As the driver leans back in her car seat the officer sees another woman sitting beside her. She looked as pale as a ghost. "What happened to her?" the officer asks.

"I don't know. She's been that way ever since we got off of Interstate 160."

*Other times we see funny or unintended signs on vehicles or on street signs:*

On a plumber's truck: "We repair what your husband fixed."

On a plumber's truck: "Don't sleep with a drip. Call your plumber."

At a tire shop in Milwaukee: "Invite us to your next blowout."

At a towing company: "We don't charge an arm and a leg. We want tows."

On an electrician's truck: "Let us remove your shorts."

In a nonsmoking area: "If we see smoke, we will assume you are on fire and take appropriate action."

At a car dealership: "The best way to get back on your feet—miss a car payment."

Outside a muffler shop: "No appointment necessary. We hear you coming."

In the front yard of a funeral home: "Drive carefully. We'll wait."

At a propane filling station, "Thank heaven for little grills."

And don't forget the sign at a Chicago radiator shop: "Best place in town to take a leak."

This collection of observations, reflections, stories and commentary will fuel your passion to do what you can to make our roads safer. Now that you've finished this book, I'm sure you'll want to read more. Hear more. And learn more. Luckily, your journey doesn't have to end here. Visit DrivingMeCrazyStories.com and read other stories, share your own and get involved in helping to make a difference.